MW00698215

CHAKRA CRYSTALS

This edition published by Shelter Harbor Press
by arrangement with Eddison Books Limited

SHELTER HARBOR PRESS
603 W 115th Street, Suite 163
New York, NY 10025
For sales, please contact: info@shelterharborpress.com

Text copyright © Kate Tomas 2006, 2019
Design copyright © Eddison Books Limited 2019
Cover artwork by Frank Duffy

All rights reserved. No part of this book may be reproduced, stored
in a retrieval system, or transmitted in any form or by any means
without the prior written permission of the publisher, nor be
otherwise circulated in any form of binding or cover other than that
in which it is published and without a similar condition, including
this condition being imposed on the subsequent purchaser.

Cataloging-in-Publication Data has been applied for
and maybe obtained from the Library of Congress.

ISBN 978-1-62795-139-5

1 3 5 7 9 10 8 6 4 2

Printed and bound in China

**This book is sold as part of the Chakra Crystals pack.
Not to be sold separately.**

CHAKRA CRYSTALS

Promote balance
and self-healing
through
crystal meditations

DR. KATE TOMAS

SHELTER HARBOR PRESS
NEW YORK

Preface

I've always found my meditative practice and work with crystals to be a sanctuary of sorts from the trauma I've survived and the oppression I live under. Historically, those most marginalized and oppressed have sought out, developed, and used alternate forms of knowing in order to empower themselves and their communities when they have been excluded from mainstream paths of power. My hope is that this book can be a small contribution to this. Even if you are working through this book on your own, know that you are not alone.

Contents

Introduction

The main aim of this book is to guide you through a process of self-development, working with crystals in a way that feels safe, easy, and enjoyable. I know from my own experience that change and transformation can be scary and challenging, so I have made this book as easy to understand and follow as possible.

The book is also intended as a practical guide to working with crystals through meditation. If you are new to any form of meditation or crystal work, it will teach you how to still your conscious mind, as well as how to unlock the healing powers of crystals, the most ancient tools of personal and spiritual development. Equally, for those who have been working with crystals for some time, the book will show you a new and rewarding way of using them.

From my experience as a professional crystal healer, I have come to know quite a lot about crystals. I work from an understanding that crystals, like plants and animals, are living beings, and you can communicate with them in order to receive information. I am always amazed by the incredible openness crystals have in sharing the knowledge they hold. They teach us how to heal ourselves physically, mentally, and emotionally, and how to develop ourselves spiritually. I know that crystals have an amazing ability to assist us on all these levels if we take the time to still our mind and consciously make contact with them. This book and the guided meditations it contains will help you do just that.

People often rely far too heavily on books that claim to tell them what certain crystals "do," or what their healing properties are. There are few books that actually encourage people to find out at first hand what a specific crystal can do for them. It is very important for you to know that by sitting quietly with a crystal, you have access to more information than you could ever get from a book; you just need to know how to access this information. The reason so many people rely on such books is simple—we are not taught to trust our intuition, our inner knowledge, or ourselves. I hope very much that, among other things, this book will give you the opportunity to develop a strong trust in yourself.

The information I have chosen to include on the healing attributes of each crystal is meant purely as a guide. The properties of the crystals have been independently experienced by people at many different times and in various places. They also reflect my own personal experiences with these crystals, so I am confident that the properties listed here are as accurate as you can get. Primarily, it is important to see these properties as a starting point, guidelines that can support your own experiences and the information you receive directly from the crystals.

How to use this book

As with most things, it is important to start at the beginning. Part One will give you a good basic understanding of how and why crystals work. In this section, you will be taught about chakras, an understanding of the human body's energy system developed thousands of years ago in what is now known as India. So much has been violently stolen from this part of the world, that it is vitally important to educate ourselves about the traditions and history of the West's use of Indian concepts. It is important to recognize that what we think of as simply part of "New Age" culture is actually a small part of a hugely complex and sophisticated philosophical understanding of the world. There is not the space for me to give you a solid grounding in Indian philosophy, but I strongly recommend reading further (*see page 142*). In Part One, you will also learn how crystals affect particular parts of the body. I believe that the more you understand about crystals and the body's energy systems, the more effective your self-healing will be.

Part Two explores the essential processes you need to complete before working with your crystals, such as cleansing, dedicating, and programming them. In Part Three, you will be introduced to meditation, and taught—in a very accessible way—how to enter an altered state of consciousness. Even if you have been meditating for many years, it is well worth reading this section, because it may teach you different techniques. I find the techniques I have given here to be the most effective and easy to follow I have come across, as do many of my clients.

From this basis, in Part Four we will move through each of the body's chakras, exploring, clearing, and healing any "blockages" we may have. For each chakra, we will meditate with one crystal, explore its healing properties, and if desired make notes about what we experience and discover on this journey. Packaged with the book are the seven crystals that we will be working with, so you can hold each crystal while you follow the guided meditations.

You may find you want to work through this book with a close friend, someone you know well and trust, or even in a small group, meeting at a set time—perhaps once a week or every two days. Whatever you decide, make sure you feel comfortable and take your time.

Each chakra treatment begins with a guided meditation for the relevant crystal. You might want to read through the meditation a couple of times first to familiarize yourself with it. Another suggestion you may find useful is to read the meditation aloud and record it, so that you can replay it and guide yourself through the meditation. Whatever you decide to do will work fine.

After each meditation, there will be an opportunity for you to write down your own notes about what you experienced and received—your feelings, thoughts, and sensations. Remember, this is your book, and the meditations are meant to become *your* meditations. It is important to write down anything you saw, felt, heard, or sensed, however strange these things may appear at the time. As you work through the book, you will come to see that the most bizarre experiences often have the most significance later on.

The final part of each chakra treatment focuses on the healing and spiritual aspects of the relevant crystal. This section is deliberately placed after the meditation so that your logical mind does not "override" what your intuition tells you; if you already "know" what a particular crystal's healing properties are, there is a danger that this knowledge will affect the meditation and what you gain from it. The logical mind is a powerful thing, constantly trying to make sense out of the experiences we have. However, it is not appropriate for what we are doing in this book.

When I have meditated with a crystal before knowing anything about it, I have always been astounded by the connections between what I naturally picked up straight from the crystal and what others have written about its healing or other properties. It is a great moment when you realize that you have actually been given some information directly from the crystal and you were right. Do not deny yourself that pleasure. It is what we are trying to encourage through this process.

Making the most of it

The most effective and powerful way to work with this book is to follow the meditations in the order they are laid out, not being tempted to jump to a particular crystal meditation or chakra because you want to work with that energy first. To get the most out of the process, it is crucial that you work through each section from the beginning right through to the end. Whether you are working alone or with a friend, you could perhaps take time each day to complete one meditation, so that within seven days you have meditated with seven crystals and explored and worked with all seven of your chakras.

If this is your first attempt at any form of meditation or work with crystals, you may feel you need longer than a day to work with each chakra. You might want to spread the work over two days or more, perhaps by completing the meditation and recording your results on one day and then returning to read about the properties of the crystal the day after. This is also fine. It may also be the case that you feel you need a day or two between meditations to let the changes initiated really settle. Ultimately, you are your own expert. No one is better qualified than you to know the speed at which you should work through the book, so trust your gut feeling and go with it. It will always be right.

The first energy center we will work with is the base chakra. This is the energy center that stabilizes us, supports us, and "grounds" us, something that is crucial in our work with crystals and to the other chakras of the body. From this starting point, we will move up through the body's energy centers, through the sacral, solar plexus, heart, throat, and brow, and finally reach our crown chakra, located just above the head.

By the time we reach this point, the energetic vibration of our body will have changed in a wholly positive way. Through working with the crystals and meditations in this structured manner, we will have achieved a new level of consciousness. Our sensitivity to all energy will have increased, and our lives will be more rewarding and in alignment with our highest good. Sounds dramatic, doesn't it? Well, it is and it isn't. You won't wake up one day and find that everything around you is different, or that you can see and hear things you weren't aware of before. However, as you work through the meditations and with the crystals, you may gradually become increasingly sensitive to the world around you; you might begin to notice what are sometimes called significant coincidences or "synchronistic events" happening in your life. You may be more and more aware of feelings, and you may make links between these feelings and situations in your life.

The closer we move toward the crown chakra, the more we reconnect with the web of energy that connects us to the rest of the universe, and the more we begin to notice this. Ultimately, the more connected we are to this web, the more we begin to understand ourselves and can change the patterns and habits that have been restricting us, often for many years. The thing to remember is that we will move only as fast as is appropriate for us. It may take years to transform the life we live now to the ideal life we dream of, or it may take a couple of months. What this book will do is help you develop yourself in the way and at the speed that are right for you. It will be an amazing journey, but one that will lead to increased happiness and progression. Enjoy it. It is meant to be fun.

From our direct experiences with the crystals through guided meditations, where we gain important information about how they can help us, we move on to put that information into practice in Part Five. Here, we will work through a proper crystal healing chakra layout as well as learn about crystal elixirs and crystal grids.

How this book came about

The information in this book came directly from the crystals themselves, just as the information you will receive for yourself will do. Perhaps like you, I realize now that I have always had unusual and special abilities. Since childhood, I have been fascinated by spiritual practice, although my family was not in any way religious. I found myself particularly drawn to studying vibration energy, "magick," and anything to do with healing. I was very sensitive to energy, good and bad, and from the age of fifteen, I was aware of hearing voices inside my head and being able to see visions and images that others could not. More than anything, I remember being incredibly aware of atmospheres and the "feelings" of places. It was not until I was seventeen, however, that I realized these voices and visions and my sensitivity to energy were what are termed "clairaudience," "clairvoyance," and "clairsentience" respectively, and it was at this point that I made a very strong connection with crystals and minerals.

Having crystals around me comforted me. I felt better, safer, and more protected when I carried my stones. I became fascinated with crystals, reading all about their healing properties and vibrations. It took many years for me to fully embrace my natural psychic and healing abilities, and a major part of that process was the two-year professional training I completed in crystal healing.

I took the crystal healing course at the same time as a full-time degree in classics, and when I finished both courses, I had a decision to make: continue with my academic studies and follow a conventional path, or take the plunge and set up as a crystal healer and oracle. I chose the latter and have now been working and meditating with crystals for many years.

When I first started meditating with crystals, my teacher would lead me through a prewritten guided meditation, much like the ones I will guide you through in this book. This allowed me to make contact with the energy of the crystal in an easy, structured way, like being taken by the hand and led through a jungle. Much later, as I developed my meditation skills through practice, I began to be able to contact the energy of the crystal almost instantly when I picked it up.

Over time, I would occasionally sit down to meditate with a crystal and almost instantly be taken into a deep meditative state. Here, I would see pictures, landscapes, and colors; hear sounds; and feel emotions and sensations. I would often hear a voice or voices "dropping" information into my mind. After perhaps ten minutes, I would come out of this state and would feel as though two or three hours had passed. I began to write down these journeys in detail, recording which crystal each journey or meditation was associated with. I noticed almost immediately that the sensations and pictures I had with each crystal correlated amazingly with that crystal's well-known healing properties.

After about a year of having these intense experiences with my crystals, I had created a large file of the most beautiful and powerful journeys imaginable. One day, I was sitting down to do my morning meditation when, instead of being taken on another voyage, I heard a voice telling me that I had to do something with the information I had received. The problem was, I had no idea what I was meant to do with these journeys. That evening, while sitting having a drink with a friend, I told them about my meditation and being told there was a purpose for this information. My friend immediately said, "Well, it's obvious, really. You need to write a book."

". . . I began to be able to contact the energy of the crystal almost instantly when I picked it up."

PART ONE

How Crystals Work

Before you start

I've always felt it is essential to have a basic understanding of what crystals are, and how they behave, in order to get the most from working with them. I'm not a scientist, but I have a basic knowledge of the way crystals grow and how they behave naturally. This has unquestionably helped to deepen my appreciation of the healing properties they hold.

In this section, we will look briefly at what crystals are and how they work. This information is not only useful but fascinating, too. As crystal healers, it does us good if we truly appreciate just what incredibly unusual beings crystals are.

A crystal's inner structure exhibits a state of perfection and balance. Everything in the universe—from planets to plants, from tables and chairs to humans and animals—is made up of tiny building blocks called atoms. The type of atoms found in an object, and how these atoms are arranged, determines its identity. This is known as atomic structure. Because of their different atomic structures, a chair is different from a cat, and a crystal is different from a plant. In chemistry and mineralogy, a crystal is a solid in which the constituent atoms are packed in a regularly ordered, repeating pattern extending in all three spatial dimensions. Unlike other objects, where the arrangement of atoms can be random or very different, crystals have a pure atomic structure throughout; they are atomically perfect.

It is this crystalline structure—the arrangement of the atoms in a repeating pattern—that is responsible for the outward shape of the crystal. All crystals belong to one of seven crystal systems. These crystal systems are based on the lines of symmetry found in crystals and are used by crystallographers (people who study the formation and growth of crystals) to categorize crystals.

The seven different crystal systems are:

1. Triclinic
2. Monoclinic
3. Orthorhombic
4. Tetragonal
5. Trigonal
6. Hexagonal
7. Cubic

For the purposes of the work we will be doing in this book, it is not really necessary for you to know any more about the seven crystal systems other than that they exist. You may come across other books that talk about cubic crystals or triclinic crystals, and you will at least now know what they are talking about.

In terms of crystal healing, the crystal system a mineral belongs to affects its vibration, as you might expect. Generally, crystals with the least axes of symmetry, such as cubic crystals, tend to act as grounding tools, whereas those with more complex atomic structures have a higher vibration, meaning they are more likely to make you feel spacey or light-headed when you meditate with them.

Crystals are used extensively in industry and can be found in many products, from watches to computers. This is because they have an amazing property. When any form of energy is applied to them, crystals generate a charge or voltage on their surface. This phenomenon is called the piezoelectric effect. In essence, this is the vibration that we crystal healers utilize to heal.

This piezoelectric effect, or the vibration of the crystal, is different for each type of crystal. The vibration of quartz, for example, will differ from that of amethyst. Crystal healers use different vibrations to treat various problems and disharmonies, because certain vibrations affect and resonate with particular parts of the physical body as well as with certain emotional energies.

When we meditate with a crystal, we are letting the vibration of the crystal affect us. It is through this vibration that we receive information, feelings, thoughts, and sensations as well as physical healing. Because all crystals of quartz, for example, have a common atomic structure, their vibration will also be common. For that reason, there will always be a similarity in the type of information and experience one has with that crystal. Three different people meditating with a piece of rose quartz might each get a different piece of information or sensation. However, their experiences would all be connected to issues concerning love and the heart, because rose quartz is a crystal that works with these issues and energies.

Crystals grow and are made in a variety of ways. The majority of crystals are very old, formed over millions of years deep below the earth's surface. Clear quartz and almost all quartz-base crystals grow naturally deep in the earth, where there are pools of silica-rich water, and where the temperature and environment are right.

Silica, the chemical that makes up quartz, is common in the earth. When these silica-rich pools of water are large, the crystals that form in them are large and clear. If, however, a crystal is growing in a confined space, it will be able to grow to only a small size. The shape of crystals is also dictated in this way. Just as potatoes grow in funny shapes when sown in rocky soil, crystals adapt their shape to their environment as they grow around the pebbles in the earth.

Other crystals are formed through intense fire and heat, like when a volcano erupts. Obsidian is such a crystal, and it is formed when the temperature inside the volcano is so hot that it melts the rocks making up the crust of the earth. These rocks may contain all kinds of crystals and minerals. When the molten rock flows down the outside of the volcano and cools, new crystals are formed. In these cases, the crystals are formed in a very short space of time, especially when compared to the millions of years often taken for quartz crystals to grow. Other crystals are also formed over many millions of years, when layer upon layer of different minerals are deposited on top of each other, forming new stones.

Beyond the scientific explanation, the work we will be embarking on with crystals will require us to have a deeper understanding of their power. It is really the experiential and so-called spiritual elements of crystals that we will be focusing on. I believe that everything that grows naturally from the earth has a spirit. Crystals are an important part of the earth and its incredible ecosystem. Through the vibration of crystals, we as humans have the ability to help bring our body into a state of perfect balance, creating health and well-being.

Crystal energy and the aura

So how do crystals affect humans? This brings us to another important element of how crystals work—connecting the vibration of crystals with the energy of the human body. It has been understood for many hundreds, perhaps thousands, of years that the human body has many different layers of energy, and that most of the time we are able to see only one part of this energy—the physical. A person's energy extends far beyond their physical body, however, and these other energies—or layers of the aura—have different names. The term "aura" is used to describe parts of the human being that cannot be seen with only the naked eye and need to be sensed or felt. Another term for these energies is "bodies," as in a physical or emotional body. You may come across spiritual writings that refer to the "emotional body" or "mental body," and this is just another term for that layer of our energy.

There is a great variety of teachings on the human aura. It is difficult to find two authors or spiritual teachers who seem to agree exactly on just how the human aura is made up. This is primarily because the aura, by nature, is always shifting and changing, and it is also possibly different for each person. What almost all people seem to agree upon, however, is that the aura is made up of different layers or levels, and that three of the most important of these layers are:

1. The emotional aura
2. The mental aura
3. The astral aura

It is helpful to imagine the human aura as being layered much like an onion—all the layers are distinct and separate and wrap tightly around each other, yet it is the combination of these layers that makes up the whole. In human energy, the physical layer is what we can see and touch; the next layer is the emotional, which we can sense on an emotional level; then comes the mental layer, which can be sensed through thoughts; and then the astral or spiritual layer, which can be sensed and communicated with when we are in a state of deep meditation.

It is helpful to see the aura illustrated to fully understand and appreciate how these different layers of energy interrelate. The layer closest to the physical body is the emotional; then comes the mental; next the astral. All of these energies have slightly different vibrations, in the same way that different crystals do. The vibration of a thought, for example, is different to the vibration of a feeling. Human energy vibrations separate and find their own levels in much the same way as oil and water.

Depending on the vibration and, therefore, its proximity to our center, or core, we will be affected by different energies to a greater or lesser extent. So it is generally the case that most people are more instantly aware of physical touch than emotional feelings; and emotional feelings have an ability to affect us more than mental thoughts. Of course, the more aware we become of these different parts of our energy, the more sensitive we are to changes in these energies. As we develop ourselves spiritually, we will aim to be aware of all layers of our aura and all parts of our energy, so that eventually we are able to sense energy affecting our astral aura, which is where we can connect with the energy of crystals.

The size and extent of the different aura layers vary from person to person and can be affected by all kind of things, from physical well-being through to the environment and thought patterns. In the following descriptions, I have given the size and extent of the different layers of the aura in a healthy person in normal conditions. I find it useful to imagine the human energy system, or aura, as an energy bubble. When we are alone, our energy bubble can extend to fill the space around us, whereas when we are with strangers—such as in a crowded elevator—our energy bubble squeezes itself in. However, if we want to connect or bond with another person, our energy can link with theirs for a short period.

This is what happens when we meet people for the first time—through different forms, although most commonly through conversation, we establish a link with that person which allows our vibrations to connect. Sometimes we feel that we connect with someone on an emotional level or maybe purely on an intellectual level. Each of these phrases describes the layer of our aura with which we are making contact with the other person. It is rare and exciting when we connect with someone on all layers of our energy, and when this happens, we often become close friends and sometimes even fall in love.

Physical layer _____

Emotional layer _____

Mental layer _____

Astral layer _____

The emotional aura

The emotional aura sits next to your physical body and extends for about an inch (2.5 cm). As you might imagine, this is where the energy of emotions is found. This is the energy you feel when you hug someone and "feel" that they are either happy or sad.

The energy of this aura is very tangible, meaning that it can be felt by almost anyone. People who are particularly empathic—meaning they have the ability to really feel what someone else may be going through emotionally—usually have a very developed awareness of their emotional body. Sometimes very empathic people can be accused by others of living too much in their emotions, and this means that most of their focus and energy is in this layer of the aura. Likewise, people who behave in a seemingly cold or unemotional way are often less connected or sensitive to this part of their energy. The ideal situation is to be in control of how and when we sense this energy; in other words, to sense this energy at all times but be in control of how we utilize this information.

The mental aura

The mental aura sits next to the emotional aura. This is where the energy of our thoughts can be found. When we think about something—whether it is a past, present, or future event—that energy sits about 2 inches (5 cm) above our physical body.

Have you ever been with someone who always seemed to be in their own thoughts? Instead of feeling things emotionally like an empathic person would, people who spend most of their time in their mental body have a tendency to think about things over and over again. Many highly intelligent people fall into this category, although not all of them. In a similar way, we have all met people who seem to lack the most basic common sense and behave in ways that display a distinct lack of thought. These people will have a weaker mental aura.

The astral aura

The astral aura, sometimes called the spiritual aura or body, is the energy body farthest away from our physical body. This is where our consciousness goes when we meditate, dream, or receive information from our spirit guides and helpers.

When we meditate, we are expanding this part of our energy to connect with the energy all around us. It is when we are fully conscious of this astral aura that we are able to feel connected to other beings, places, and times. All of this occurs while in a meditative state. This layer of the aura is of great importance to us while working with crystals, because it is through the expansion of this energy that we can connect with the energy of the crystals. Regular meditation can increase consciousness of this aura and strengthen its energy. By the time we finish working through this book, your astral aura will clear and strong.

Becoming aware of your aura

Becoming more sensitive to the different layers of our aura should ideally be a process that grows naturally and gradually, but it can also happen quickly. Many of my clients come to me for help because, for a variety of reasons, they have become rapidly aware of their emotional body or aura. This may occur through trauma, loss, or even incredible experiences, such as falling in love.

Some people spend most of their lives really aware of only their physical body or aura; they feel emotions, but usually in a limited way. A sudden experience that makes them aware of a whole other part of their being can be quite a shock. People can become what is often termed "oversensitive," meaning that they feel all emotions around them very intensely, whether their own or not. Crystals can be useful in situations such as this, helping to integrate the new-found emotional sensitivity with the rest of the person's energy, and allowing for the body to become more balanced in the way it senses energy.

When someone becomes more aware of their energy and its different layers, they tend to become more sensitive in all ways. Take, for example, a person who has always been truly aware or conscious of their physical body. If they fall in love, they will find that even their physical sensations are heightened as they become more sensitive generally. That's why when we touch someone we love, we get those shivers down our body; this is a very physical reaction to our strong sensitivity to the emotional aura.

When we work with crystals on the astral layer of our aura, the benefit will be felt through all the layers of our energy. If you imagine that when we connect with, and are affected by, the energy of the crystals on the astral level, this energy will filter down through our spiritual senses to our mental aura, allowing for us to think differently. Then it will affect our emotional aura, opening us to deeper sensations and sensitivities of emotions, and finally reach our physical aura, where it will strengthen and improve our body. Throughout all of this, the energy or vibration of the crystal we are working with will not only be strengthening each layer of energy it passes through; it will also be releasing any blockages held in each layer and healing any problems, whether they be astral, mental, emotional, or physical.

Chakra energy

Possibly the most important part of the human energy system—certainly for our purposes in this book—is the chakra system. Developed many thousands of years ago in India, the chakra system we hear so much about today has its roots in an ancient and rigorous spiritual tradition, which many New Age teachers have barely explored. Most of the current Western knowledge of the chakra system is derived from an English translation of Sanskrit texts from the tenth and

THE LOCATION OF THE CHAKRAS

Crown chakra

Brow chakra

Throat chakra

Heart chakra

Solar plexus chakra

Sacral chakra

Base chakra

sixteenth centuries, although the seven chakras we will be working with in this book were first described nearly 2,600 years ago in the ancient sacred texts of the *Yoga Upanishads*.

For our work with crystals, we need only a good, basic understanding of the chakras; where each one is located and how they affect our energy. The original Sanskrit word, *çakra*, with the "ç" pronounced as "ch," means "wheel." If you could see energy, you would be able to perceive that the energy emanating from the chakras spins like a wheel. There are considered to be seven major chakras, sometimes referred to as energy centers. In English, they are named after their location on the human body: the base (at the base of the spine), the sacral (just below the navel), the solar plexus, the heart, the throat, the brow, and the crown (at the top of the head).

The location of the first five chakras has a corresponding main nerve ganglion on the spinal column, and the top two (the brow and crown chakras) correspond with the two main parts of the brain (upper and lower). In medical terms, a ganglion is a group of nerve cells forming a nerve center, specifically one located outside the brain or spinal cord. It is a center of power, activity, or energy. We can see, therefore, that the seven main chakras are locations not only of spiritual, emotional, and mental energy and power, but also of physical energy.

The chakras are incredibly important parts of our being. Our bodies are made up of vibrating matter, and our chakras are centers for this vibrating energy. If the vibration of one or more of our chakras is out of balance, this can, over time, lead to physical, emotional, or mental problems. The term "disease" literally means "dis-ease" or a lack of comfort and ease. Keeping our seven chakras clear and vibrating at their ideal frequency will create a strong sense of health and balance on all levels: emotional, spiritual, mental, and physical. Understanding the relationships between our subtle bodies such as our auras and chakras can significantly improve our quality of life and prevent illness and disease.

It is important to understand a little about each of the seven major chakras. In the text that follows you will find details of each chakra, the energy they govern, and their corresponding physical influences.

The base chakra

EARTH • PHYSICAL IDENTITY • SURVIVAL • BASIC INSTINCTS

Located at the base of the spine, this chakra is our energetic foundation. It is here that we can connect to the earth and feel grounded and safe. Through working with the base chakra, we can stabilize our energy and enjoy a good healthy relationship with our physical body.

The base chakra is associated with all things physical and practical. This energy center needs to be working well and in balance for us to have great physical health, financial prosperity, and security. People who are considered to be down-to-earth have strong, balanced base chakras. The color associated with the base chakra is red, a vibrant, strong color. Red has the longest wavelength and the slowest vibration of all colors in the visible spectrum.

It is very important to have a balanced and open base chakra, especially when working with the energy of crystals and meditating, because our link to the earth through this chakra provides a strong foundation for our spiritual growth. It may be useful to imagine human energy as the branches and roots of a tree. A tree can grow only as tall as its roots can grow down. A tree's roots usually extend as far underground as the branches spread in the crown. If we were able to see a full-grown tree with its roots exposed, we would perceive that what we see above ground is reflected almost exactly below.

Like the roots of a tree, the base chakra anchors us in the physical world, making us feel grounded. By being fully connected to the real world and the earth, our energetic roots absorb energy. If our base chakra is not fully clear, balanced, and clean, then we will be restricted in how much we can develop our other chakras. For this reason, it is important to recognize the base chakra as the gateway to unlocking the energy and potential of all the other chakras. Each chakra is associated with different parts of the physical body, and the base chakra is connected with the parts that support ourselves—our legs, bones, and feet.

The sacral chakra

WATER • CREATIVITY IN ALL FORMS • SEXUALITY • ENERGY

The second chakra is called the sacral because it is found near the sacrum on the spine, located in the abdomen about three fingers down from the navel. The location of the sacral chakra is significant, because it is where the embryo grows in a pregnant person. After the base, the sacral chakra is the next energy center to work on in order to achieve great personal and spiritual development.

This energy center is related to the element of water and to all forms of creative energy, including reproduction and sexuality. It connects us to others through feeling, desire, sensation, and movement. When working correctly, balanced, and clean, this chakra brings us fluidity, the ability to adapt to our changing surroundings, depth of feeling, and sexual fulfillment. It is this chakra that relates to creativity in all its forms, whether that be through artistic expression, creative writing, making something physically, or procreation.

For this reason, the sacral chakra is connected to human sexuality. Someone with a balanced, open, and clean sacral chakra will have a healthy sexual appetite, or libido, and will be confident and happy with their sexuality. For many, especially women, trans, and nonbinary people, the sacral chakra is the energy center that has had to process the most trauma and requires the most work to unblock and maintain clear. This is not a failure, but instead a symptom of living in a culture where rape, sexual assault, and harassment as well as cis-heteronormativity dominates. For those of us who are survivors of sexual assault, the sacral chakra is often blocked or unbalanced. Symptoms of an unbalanced sacral chakra include associating sex with guilt, pain, or negativity, and feeling shy or awkward around discussions of sex or near people to whom one is attracted.

The sacral chakra is also strongly linked with self-confidence and vitality. When it is working properly, we feel strong, healthy, and confident about our thoughts, actions, and generally who we are. The energy of the sacral chakra is trusting, innocent, and joyful, energy that we often lose on the journey to adulthood. By working consciously with the sacral chakra, we can regain some of that youthful joy and creativity.

The color associated with this chakra is orange, a vibrant, joyful, and creative color. Orange is the color of fire and light. Brighter than the red associated with the base chakra, orange is the color of energy, vitality, and optimism.

The solar plexus chakra

FIRE • IDENTITY • POWER • SELF-DEFINITION • ANXIETY

Like many of the chakras, the solar plexus chakra gets its name from its location. Sitting just above the navel, and between the two parts of the rib cage, it is here that our issues to do with personal power, will, and autonomy are centered. When we are nervous or emotionally uncomfortable about something, we feel it in the solar plexus. Have you ever felt sick to your stomach due to nerves? That is the energy of your solar plexus going into spasm—the chakra literally opens and closes very quickly as our emotional body tries to deal with a situation that causes us great worry and anxiety. When we get a shock, such as a loud noise or someone jumping out at us suddenly, the rush of energy and adrenalin we feel through our body centers on our solar plexus.

The solar plexus is the chakra associated with our personal power, so any situation that potentially threatens our personal power—whether emotionally or physically—immediately triggers an energetic response from this part of the body. It is through this energy center that we feel things and sense energies. For example, have you ever walked into a room full of people and picked up on the "atmosphere"? Sometimes we can enter a particular place and just "know" that the people in there are happy, or that an argument recently took place. When we pick up on atmospheres or energies, we are sensing a change in our energy environment through our solar plexus.

Some people, called clairsentients, have very open and sensitive solar plexus chakras. This means they have the ability to "sense" how another person is feeling, even if they are not physically near, and sometimes even "feel" certain events happening before they occur.

When our solar plexus is very open and able to pick up a lot of external energies, we feel the need to protect ourselves. Everyone has had an experience of instinctively crossing their arms over the front of their body when they feel nervous or threatened in some way. When we do this, we are covering our solar plexus, preventing it from picking up any more negative energy.

People who have experienced disordered eating are, among other things, dealing with a sensitivity of the solar plexus. When we feel a lack of control over the energy we pick up on and are sensitive to, it will affect our digestion, our hunger messages, and will cause us to desperately try to control the energy in this area of our physical body. Many clients of mine who have experienced disordered eating describe a real sense of having large parts—or all—of their lives dictated by others, whether it be their parents, siblings, partner, agent, boss, or their children.

When we feel out of control of our solar plexus, we try to take control over one of the few things we alone have responsibility for—what goes into our body. Ultimately, this method of controlling the energy of the solar plexus is not effective and leads to great physical and emotional damage, but when the energy centers of the body are so completely out of balance, we will try anything to create a change.

When healthy, the solar plexus brings us energy, spontaneity, and nondominating power. We feel in control of our lives and our destinies, and we have a healthy relationship with food.

"When we pick up on atmospheres or energies, we are sensing a change in our energy environment through our solar plexus."

The heart chakra

AIR • SOCIAL IDENTITY • LOVE • SELF-ACCEPTANCE AND SELF-LOVE

The heart chakra is found in the middle of the chest, a little lower down the body than where the physical heart is found. The primary concerns of the heart chakra are love: universal, selfless love; pure, strong compassion; and love between individuals. This chakra is often not fully open or balanced. It is my belief that a lot of people are born with a naturally open heart chakra, and that through a variety of experiences— primarily during childhood—we learn to close our hearts to some extent. Many children learn from the adults around them that to have an open heart is a bad and dangerous thing (and, to a large extent, they are right).

Such lessons are not always taught intentionally. I don't think that most parents intend for their children to close down their heart chakra. Instead, social conditioning and early childhood experiences can make us feel that to be open-hearted is dangerous. There is no doubt that having, and living with, a fully open and functioning heart chakra makes you vulnerable, and whether we like it or not, the world we live in is not a safe or kind place. It is not possible to go through life with a fully opened heart chakra, but rather than seeing vulnerability as something to be avoided at all costs, in an ideal world we would discern when it is safe to be open-hearted and have the capacity to open our hearts at will. Ultimately, I believe that it is only when we are truly vulnerable that we are open to experiencing pure love and ultimate peace. When our heart chakra is not in balance, we will feel disconnected from the rest of the world and become withdrawn and often angry. When we speak of someone having a broken heart, we are describing the energy of their heart chakra being disrupted or damaged in some way.

Sometimes, people with physical heart problems have a long history of emotional trauma and "heartbreak" that has been suppressed. Any physical problems relating to the heart, or to the circulation and blood, are linked to the energy of the heart chakra and to the circulation of love.

As the fourth chakra, the heart chakra is the energy center between the lower three (base, sacral, and solar plexus) and the top three (throat, brow, and crown). Without the heart chakra being fully balanced and open, real development of the spiritual centers of the throat, brow, and crown is not possible. In this way, the heart acts like a kind of filter, allowing for true mastery of spiritual abilities only to people with open hearts. If someone's heart is not open and balanced, there will be a distinct and clear limit to the accuracy and power of any spiritual work they do, no matter how hard they try or how naturally gifted they may be. Even if their top three chakras are open and functioning well, none of this energy can pass through the heart center to be made manifest through the solar plexus, sacral, and base chakras. We must work with our hearts open! I have been working as a psychic for nearly twenty years, and one of the most important rules I have established in my practice is that I will not work for or with anyone I don't feel safe to have a fully open heart with. Without an open heart chakra, my work is significantly reduced in accuracy and value. This rule has had a knock-on effect of protecting me.

Ultimately, like all the chakras, the heart opens and balances itself naturally the more it is used, although we can also go through dramatic and instantaneous heart-opening experiences. These affect us much as when we first become aware of our emotional aura (*see page 23*), and a heart-opening and awareness of the emotional body often occur concurrently. Falling in love for the first time is possibly one of the best examples of a dramatic and powerful heart-opening experience. Receiving pure healing or experiencing a true connection to the

Divine—either through your own meditation or through another person—opens, balances, and heals the heart chakra.

Having an open heart does not mean you are overemotional or let yourself be abused by others. Instead, it means you make every decision, take every action, and say every word with the intention of being loving. Having an open heart makes you vulnerable in the sense that you become harmless—not a threat to anyone. Of course, it is not always appropriate or safe to make oneself harmless, and the circumstances where one person is safe to have an open heart will be a circumstance where it is absolutely not safe for someone else to. Structural oppressions; racism, sexism, cissexism, homophobia, ableism, and classism all mean that for each of us, the circumstances whereby we feel safe to open our hearts are radically different. Be wary of anyone telling you that the only way is love—maybe for them, but not for us all.

The throat chakra

SOUND • CREATIVE IDENTITY • SELF-EXPRESSION

The throat chakra is, unsurprisingly, located at the center of the throat. This energy center is primarily associated with communication and all forms of expression: talking, shouting, and singing. It also regulates creative energy and is in this way linked directly with the energy of the sacral chakra.

Neither the throat nor the sacral chakra can be in balance without the other. If you think about it, the throat is the chakra that allows for the expression of the creative energy built and created by the sacral chakra. If there is a lack of creative (sacral) energy, perhaps manifesting as writer's block or a lack of inspiration or motivation, then the throat chakra will be unable to perform its role of expressing this energy. Likewise, if the throat chakra is blocked or congested—say, for example, because you are putting off discussing something challenging with someone—then no matter how much creative ability or energy is built up by the sacral chakra, none of it will be able to be made to manifest, because it cannot be expressed. It is not only the energy of the sacral chakra that will be affected by an imbalanced throat chakra, because the throat is the point of expression for all of the energy centers.

The throat chakra is also about vibration and sound. It is at the throat that we make our sounds; it is where we create the noises that let us communicate with others and be understood. Babies are born with pure, clear, open chakras, and the throat is no exception. We are born with a fully functioning throat, because our ability to make noise is fundamental to survival.

It is essential that the throat center is working well and clearly; otherwise we will not only be restricted in our ability to express our creativity, but we will also be limited in our relationships with others.

Many people have an underactive or congested throat chakra without even being aware of it. The common cold—especially its companion, the sore throat—is a classic symptom of a slight to severe throat chakra imbalance. Like all chakras, with the exception of the heart, the throat can be overactive as well as congested. Have you ever met someone who *never* stops talking? People who spend a large amount of time talking, often about mundane and unimportant issues, tend to have more of a problem with their throat chakra than those of us who occasionally find it difficult to speak out.

The brow chakra

LIGHT • SELF-REFLECTION • CLARITY OF VISION • PERCEPTION • THOUGHT

The brow chakra is located between the eyebrows on the forehead. It is associated with the color indigo, a very deep blue, much like a midnight sky. This is the energy center that regulates and controls all of our vision—not just our physical vision but our intuitive vision, too. In almost all known ancient cultures, the intuitive sense was as important as physical vision, and the brow chakra was named the "third eye."

Perception is important, because it dictates how we think about a situation or event and, therefore, determines our response to it. How we perceive something is another way of saying how we think about it, and the brow chakra is associated with thought. For this reason, it is important that the brow chakra is in a state of balance; if it is not, then our view of situations—how we think and analyze events and experiences— can become clouded and unbalanced.

The brow chakra is also the center of our psychic abilities and power. In our modern Western culture, we are taught to close down this receptor of energy and, if it can't or won't be closed down, not to speak about it at all. The ironic thing about this is that for many years, governments of various countries have been utilizing the psychic power of some people's third eye to gain information that they would not otherwise have access to. Called remote viewing, this particular type of ability is nothing more than a focused development and opening of the brow chakra.

When we live with an unbalanced brow chakra, we incur all kinds of challenges, ranging from difficulty in being objective through to serious headaches or migraines and physical vision problems.

It is important to recognize that not everyone will have the same abilities. Psychic abilities are not limited to "vision," and so, although we speak about the third eye, we mean eye in the metaphorical sense. Clairsentience, which we spoke about in regard to the solar plexus (*see page 32*), is also a strong psychic ability, and in this way is an energy linked to the brow chakra. There is also claircognizance—clear knowing, the ability to "just know" something. Many people have experienced knowing who was going to ring before the phone rang, or even knowing who would be at the door before they opened it.

When the brow chakra is open, clear, balanced, and healthy, it allows for strong, vivid dreams to occur and enables us to remember them. We are also able to view situations in which we are involved in a balanced and healthy way. Our physical vision will improve and our natural psychic abilities will increase.

"The brow chakra is also the center of our psychic abilities and power."

The crown chakra

SPIRIT • CONNECTION

The crown chakra is the energy center that connects you to everything. Whatever you believe about God, spirit guides, and the universe, the crown chakra lets you feel connected to something. Many people identify this feeling with a devotion to a particular religion, god, or goddess. Others feel connected strongly to the natural world, plants, or animals. Some feel a strong spiritual connection and affinity to the mineral kingdom: crystals.

Each of these individual connections is just a single manifestation or facet of the rest of the universe. The crown energy center is our connection to the greater world beyond, to a timeless, limitless space. When we meditate upon the connection the crown chakra brings, we can experience pure bliss; the feeling of being completely held, safe, and part of an incredible, beautiful "being."

For centuries, spiritual masters have focused upon the crown chakra as the gateway to enlightenment. Because the crown chakra is the connection to our source—whatever you believe that is—we experience true liberation when we consciously raise our awareness and focus to that point, and away from the mundane, practical, and physical concerns of our lives.

The crown chakra can only be fully opened and worked with when all of the other chakras are in perfect balance and harmony, because we need to be fully grounded—to be completely healthy, energywise—to work with the energy to which this chakra can give us access. Many people who are new to spiritual development—especially in New Age circles—are so desperate to open their crown chakra that they don't do any of the groundwork on the other six chakras, instead focusing entirely upon the crown. You may have met people who always seem to be on another planet, totally ungrounded and very "airy-fairy," or lacking common sense. Those who spend hours meditating, trying to open their crowns, trying hard to "see" or "hear" amazing spiritual truths, have a hard time living in the real world.

Clairvoyants and clairaudients must take great care not to push their crown chakra too much. The nature of our work means that we receive information through our crown chakra. If we are not careful, it is all too easy to be tempted into pushing for more and more information, for sharper and clearer voices or visions, without developing our other energy centers accordingly. Just like anyone else, if our crown chakra connection is stretched without the required work on the other chakras, we run the risk of believing we hold the answers to all questions and have knowledge of all things. This leads to great self-importance and pride, the complete opposite of true enlightenment.

I know of a great many psychics who have fallen into the trap of not working on themselves and fail to ensure their own chakras are clear and balanced before trying to advise others spiritually. As we learned in the section on the base chakra (see page 28), our spiritual branches can reach only as high as our roots reach low, and, if our chakras are congested or unbalanced in any way, the information we have access to will similarly be limited. Some of the information these people receive may be accurate, but as a whole the energy will be unbalanced and impure. Sadly, it is so often people like this who give other, much more conscientious, psychics a bad name.

When the crown chakra is balanced, healthy, and open to an appropriate level, people feel an amazing sense of well-being and health, and they feel totally connected to all existence. They become very aware, even blissful. To have a fully open and healthy crown chakra requires all of the other chakras to be healthy, and this is a great achievement. And it is for this reason that it is a rare phenomenon.

PART TWO

Preparation

Choosing your crystals

How you go about acquiring your crystals is important, because it affects how the crystals are used and the kind of energy attached to them. When we buy a crystal, there will always be a purpose behind the purchase. Often you will know exactly why you are buying a crystal: it may be to use as a piece of jewelry; it may be for a birthday present; and sometimes you may not know consciously what that purpose is. What I will teach you here is how to go about selecting exactly the right crystal for your purpose.

Making the right choice of crystal is important, because some crystals will work better with you than others. Often I have been in a crystal store and felt especially attracted and drawn to a particular stone, and yet felt nothing toward its neighbor, even though they were the same mineral, the same size, and the same shape.

Because all crystals are unique, each has its own spirit and particular energy. Some crystals will be more compatible with your energy at a particular time. It always amazes me how people are able to draw to them exactly the crystals they need. Whenever I teach, I give each student a collection of specific crystals that they will work with throughout the course. At the beginning of the first morning, the bags of crystals—all containing the same minerals—are placed in the middle of the circle of students. I then ask them to take the bag they are most drawn to. Without exception—and I have been teaching for many years—every single person is drawn to, and chooses, a different bag from the others. A situation has never arisen where two people both felt attracted to one bag of crystals.

What this shows is that even when blindly choosing crystals—that is, not being able to choose each crystal in a selection—you will always end up with the crystals you were meant to have and work with. The crystals you have in front of you were chosen in just that way; even though you were unable to select each individual stone, rest assured that the collection of minerals you need—and that want to work with you—are the ones you have in your package. This works even if someone bought the package for you as a gift—the package was intended for you, so your crystals would have been chosen appropriately.

With all methods of crystal selection, the intention you set is of the greatest importance. What this means is that, before you decide which crystal you need, you set the clear intention that you will find exactly the one you require. You can do this silently in your head, almost like asking yourself, your higher self, or the universe to make sure you are led to the right stone. If I needed a crystal to help me concentrate on writing, for example, I would close my eyes and ask that I find such a stone, then go about choosing my crystal. This ensures you always get the crystal you need. If you're not sure why you need a particular stone, that's fine; just ask that you find the crystal you need and leave it at that.

Scanning for a crystal

When you are intentionally choosing a crystal for yourself, there are three main ways to find out which crystal to choose. The first is called scanning. This is a useful technique when you have a large selection of crystals to choose from and are unsure which stone is the right one for you. It works by utilizing the astral layer of your aura to sense and identify your chosen stone.

To scan for a crystal, hold your hand over the selection of crystals, 2 to 3 inches (5–7 cm) above them, and gently and slowly pass it over the stones. What you are doing here is feeling the energy of the crystals with your energy. You are tuning in to their vibration. When you pass your hand over the stone that is right for you at that time, you will feel a slight tingle, some heat or cold, or you will just "know" that this stone is the one.

Some people think that you should use only your nondominant hand for scanning—your left hand if you are right-handed, and your right hand if you are left-handed. I have never found this to be particularly helpful advice, because I have always scanned with my right hand and am definitely right-handed. See how you feel. If one hand feels more sensitive to the energy of the crystals, then use that one.

To be able to scan successfully takes time and practice. Although we all have the ability to sense immediately which stone is right for us, we often are not practiced at recognizing this sensation. Whatever your reaction, the stone that first draws you to it while your hand is hovering above it is your stone. As you grow more confident in your choices, scanning will become easier and quicker to do.

Using your intuition

Another method for choosing your crystals is similar to scanning but less conspicuous, which is handy if you don't fancy getting strange looks from people as you pass your hands over all the crystals in a store. Just like scanning, this technique simply requires you to focus on the purpose for which you want the crystal, or that you ask to be drawn to the correct crystal, and to close your eyes. Let your eyes pass back and forth under your eyelids, and when you feel ready open your eyes. The crystal you see first when you open your eyes will be the one you need. It's as simple as that. This technique utilizes your intuition, the part of your unconscious that knows what you need.

Using crystal cards

The third way of identifying the crystal you need is by using specially designed crystal cards. There are many of these cards on the market at the moment—I have three different packs myself. These cards each have the name of a different crystal written on them, and the accompanying booklet usually gives information about the healing properties of the stones. I don't tend to use these booklets, although some of them can be good. Instead, I like to take the cards and shuffle them, and once I have set my clear intention to find the right crystal, I choose a card. Then I find out as much as possible from the crystal by meditating with the card. When I first became interested in crystals, I found that this method was very effective, especially when the pack of cards contained a comprehensive range of crystals, some of which I hadn't heard of before.

Other ways to choose crystals

There are many other ways of choosing crystals. As you become more attuned to the energy of crystals, you may find you dream about them. I often have vivid dreams where I am surrounded by a large amount of a particular crystal. In one dream, at a time when I was going through a lot of heart chakra change and trauma, I dreamed that a large turquoise necklace was hanging around my neck. I remember feeling incredibly safe and held by having this stone near to my heart, and when I awoke I knew I just had to work with that particular crystal. I bought myself a turquoise necklace that morning.

Sometimes a friend will just give you a crystal for no particular reason. One of my best friends, the amazingly talented artist and musician Natalie Shaw, seems to give me a crystal each time I see her. Natalie travels all over the world performing, and so some of the crystals I have from Nat have come from exotic places. It always amazes me that whenever I receive a crystal gift from her, it is exactly what I need at that time. Nat describes how a particular crystal told her it was for me, and sure enough, when I hold it, I feel significantly better. Your close friends can be just as tuned in to which crystals you need as you are, and sometimes even more so.

For this reason, choosing a crystal for another person is easy. You just hold the intention in your mind of finding a crystal for a particular person, and use one of the above techniques for choosing it.

Cleansing your crystals

Once you have chosen your crystals, such as the seven crystals that came with this book, you need to prepare them for work. Here, I will explain the main methods for cleansing your crystals to remove any negative or unnecessary energy from them.

Cleansing is probably one of the most important practices for anyone working with crystals. All too often, when crystals don't seem to be having the desired effect for someone, it is because they are dirty. I don't mean just physically dirty, as in being dusty or sticky, but energetically dirty. All things can accumulate negativity, including heavy energy, such as sadness, fear, or anger, or any negative emotion or feeling. Crystals are especially absorbent, because they are carriers and transmitters of energy. When you get a crystal for the first time, you don't know where it has been and what it has experienced.

It is useful to think of negative energy as being like dust; it is all around us, and if a room or an item in that room is not cleansed regularly, dust can accumulate. Negative energy is created when we argue, get angry, or cry. It hangs around until it is cleared out. This cleansing process is called space-clearing, and it can be done in a variety of ways. Often, space-clearing techniques are similar to the methods I will teach you for cleansing crystals, and it is well worth finding out more about these so you can keep your home energetically clean and clear.

The main methods I use for cleansing crystals are based on the five elements: earth, air, fire, water, and spirit. When using crystals, I find it excellent practice to work with the elements, because crystals are completely natural beings. I also believe that cleansing methods should be as simple as possible. In my long experience, I have rarely found crystals to need complex, involved methods of cleansing.

Cleansing with the earth element

The first cleansing method involves the element of earth and is based on the idea of returning the crystal to its natural habitat—the earth itself. Because this method takes longer than some of the others, I use this technique when I feel my crystals need an extra boost. It's almost like giving them a short break at a spa.

1. Identify a safe place in your yard where you know you won't be disturbed. Make sure the space you use is actually yours—I wouldn't recommend burying your crystals in a public park or garden, because you never know who else could find them.

2. Dig a hole in the ground 5 to 6 inches (12–15 cm) deep. As you do so, ask the earth to clean, refresh, and recharge your crystals.

3. Place your crystals in the hole and cover them with soil. Remember to place a marker of some kind in the ground to remind you where you buried them. It may seem excessively cautious to do so—especially if you intend to leave your crystals in the ground only overnight—but believe me, I have spent hours searching for seemingly easy-to-find buried crystals, and I wouldn't recommend it. You need to leave the crystals buried for at least twelve hours to clean them fully. It's best to leave them for up to a week, because, much like humans, the longer a break they get, the better they feel afterward. More than a week is unnecessary, and I have not noticed any difference in crystals left buried for a week and those left for a month. Use your intuition to judge how long to leave them in.

4. Once you're ready to collect them from their short break, carefully dig them up. I always use my bare hands, because there is no risk of damaging the crystals with a sharp instrument, but also because it gives me the opportunity to feel connected to the earth itself. You may need to dust them off, or even rinse them if you are sure they are not water soluble.

Cleansing with the air element

The next two methods for cleansing utilize the element of air: smudging with white sage and using what is known as the "sacred breath."

SMUDGING WITH WHITE SAGE

Smudging with dried white sage is possibly my favorite way of cleaning my crystals, because it is a thorough method and I feel involved in the process. Dried white sage has been used for hundreds of years by Native Americans to clear space and purify sacred objects. By burning the end of a wand of white sage and letting the smoke pass through and around every part of a room or object, any negative energy is cleared away. There is actually some science behind the effectiveness of white sage; the smoke it produces is full of negative ions.

Negative ions are found in abundance in nature in places, such as waterfalls, forests, and beaches. These are molecules found in the air that have lost all their electrical charge. They have been proven to filter out impurities in the air and increase the flow of oxygen to the brain, resulting in higher levels of alertness and more mental energy. Negative ions are the opposite of the positive ions produced by electrical equipment, such as smartphones and computers. Because opposite ions attract, the negative ions draw to them all impurities, which clump together where they are heavy enough to fall to the ground.

White sage smoke also clears away energetic impurities, such as anger, fear, greed, and hate. For this reason, smudging with white sage is a great method for cleansing crystals. First, find a small, flame-proof dish that you can use exclusively for smudging. Traditionally, an abalone shell was used, because it is naturally heat-proof and represented the element of water, but you can use an ashtray or any little bowl.

White sage is usually sold wrapped tightly into a bundle tied with colored cotton thread. You can light the end of this bundle (called a stick), or else, as I often do, loosen the thread a little and pull out a stick of sage. I find that the sage burns much better this way; if it is too tightly bound, not enough oxygen can get to it. Some bundles work perfectly in the way they have been bound; see what works best for you.

Light the end of the sage, making sure you are holding it over the bowl. You will need to blow the flame out as soon as it is alight and let the sage smoke. A lot of ash will be created, and it can be really hot— hot enough to burn a carpet, as I have found to my peril—so always make sure you have a bowl underneath to catch any falling ash.

Once the sage is smoking, pass your crystals—one at a time— through the smoke, visualizing any negativity being washed away with the smoke. It's as simple as that. Use your intuition here, as always when working with crystals, because some crystals will want to be held in the smoke for a long time—maybe even a few minutes—whereas others will be happy with a quick whip-through. Trust your judgment—you will know when your crystal is clean.

THE SACRED BREATH

This is the other cleansing method connected to the element of air, and it involves a very clear focus of attention. I use this method most often, because it is almost instant, requires no equipment or special space, and is effective. I clean my crystals like this between clients when I don't have time to cleanse them with sage or using any of the other methods, and it does the job well. Having said that, about once a week, I also cleanse the crystals I work with using one of the other, more thorough methods. This is because the effectiveness of the sacred breath depends upon the purity of your intention.

First, center yourself and set a clear intention to clear away any negative or unnecessary energy with your breath. Then, holding your crystal in your hand, blow sharply onto the stone three times, imagining the negativity as dust that you're blowing away. This is an effective method if done correctly. It is based on the understanding that breath is a sacred material, because it is our breath that gives us life, and that this breath can be charged or programmed for a specific purpose. Much like when we blow a kiss, we are using our breath as a vehicle for our affection, and here we are using the breath as a vehicle for cleansing energy.

The following cleansing methods utilize the elements of fire and water to clean away negativity from the crystals. Unlike the methods described above, which can be used with all crystals, not all stones can be cleansed in the following ways; some crystals are sensitive to heat or water and you may even destroy them. If in any doubt, don't use the fire or water cleansing methods.

Cleansing with the fire element

This method is simple but effective. You will need a pure white candle set in a stable candle holder. It is important that the candle be bought with the purpose of crystal cleansing in mind and is used only for this purpose. Light the candle and, being careful not to burn your fingers, pass the crystal through the flame. This may sound like a violent way of cleansing, but in my experience a lot of crystals really seem to love it, because it quickly and effectively burns off any negativity. You will find that passing crystals through the flame will leave some of them with a black film on their surface. This can usually be wiped off if you want to get rid of it, but it is not necessary— although the crystal may look more physically dirty after this method, it is clean energetically.

Crystals that definitely should not be cleansed using the fire method include hematite, boji stones, and any crystals that have a metal as a constituent, because they conduct heat well and will burn both you and their resting place. Opals must never be taken anywhere near a flame, because they contain water, which, if burned away, would turn a valuable opal into a plain piece of agate. Instead, opals respond especially well to being cleansed in water.

Cleansing with the water element

Water is often used for cleaning crystals, yet it can do a lot of damage. I use water as a cleansing method occasionally, but only if I am sure that it will not do any harm. Many minerals are water soluble, meaning that if you leave them in water long enough, they will dissolve. However, some crystals—and almost all quartz-based minerals—respond well to the occasional water cleanse. If your crystal is dirty physically as well as energetically, cleaning in water is especially good.

It is best to use special water that has come from a sacred well or holy place for cleansing crystals. For many years, I lived in Glastonbury, and I would always bring my crystals to be cleansed in the beautiful Chalice Well, holding each one under the stream of water until I felt they were clean. If I couldn't get to the well itself, I used water I had collected from the well and soaked my crystals in it overnight. If you don't have access to such a perfect location for crystal cleansing, don't worry—you can clean your crystals under running tap water, holding them in the flowing water and visualizing any negativity flowing away down the drain. I recommend this method of cleansing to a lot of my clients, because they can cleanse their crystals quickly and easily this way. Just remember to check that your crystal is safe in water. Some crystals that should never be cleansed in water are celestite, malachite, and salt—it seems obvious, but I have known someone to clean their large, expensive salt crystal in a bowl of water overnight.

Dedicating and programming your crystals

There is a lot of confusion about the difference between dedicating and programming crystals. I hope to explain clearly the differences between them here, and to show you how to go about performing both techniques. As far as I am concerned, the dedication and programming of crystals is essential practice for anyone working with crystals. In essence, dedication is a method or ritual whereby a crystal is set up to work in only a positive way. Programming is asking the crystal, in a specific way, to work to achieve a particular aim.

Once you have cleansed your crystal, you need to dedicate it. All crystals that pass through your hands need to be dedicated to be used with only good intention. This ensures that, whatever happens to the crystal after it leaves you—whether that be in a couple of hours or many years—it can never be used to harm anyone or anything. Although crystals themselves are deeply loving beings, they are also transmitters of energy; therefore, they can, if used in the wrong way, have a negative effect. Dedication not only prevents intentional misuse of the crystal but also protects against any major damage being done unintentionally.

The dedication I use is simple and powerful. To dedicate a crystal, simply hold it in your cupped hands and repeat in your head, or out loud if you prefer, "I dedicate you to be used with only loving energies." If the crystal is too big or heavy to hold, place your hands above it.

Repeat this until you feel that the crystal has been fully dedicated. That may take one repetition or it may take ten. I usually find that three times is enough for most stones. And that's it. After you have dedicated your crystal to working with only loving energies, you can rest assured that no harm will come to anyone through that crystal.

Programming is the next stage. This is very different to dedication, because when we program a crystal, we are asking it to work with us to achieve a particular aim. You could, for example, ask your crystal to help you heal yourself. Hold the crystal in your hand, in the same way as for dedication. Again, if it is too big or heavy to hold, place your hands above it. Mentally or out loud, ask that the crystal to work with you in a particular way. Continue to repeat your request until you feel the crystal has understood.

I tend to be as specific as possible with my programming, because you can always change your program at another point. To do this, you just cleanse the crystal in the usual way, with the express intention of cleansing it of any program you may no longer need.

". . . dedication is a method or ritual whereby a crystal is set up to work in only a positive way."

PART THREE

Working with Your Crystals

How to meditate

In essence, meditation is nothing more than focusing your attention on one thing to the exclusion of everything else. In the Indian tradition, the breath is focused upon to the exclusion of all else. What this does is make one acutely aware of nothing but the present moment; this is what mindfulness means. To some extent, when we watch television or focus on one of those "magic eye" pictures, we are, in effect, meditating. For many people, however, meditation involves a conscious decision to sit or lie down and actively connect to a source of higher knowledge.

When we meditate, we open ourselves to receiving higher guidance. This guidance can come in the form of symbols, pictures, words, or sentences. It can also come as pure knowledge, when information or a "knowing" just pops into our mind while we are in meditation. There are many different theories on where this information or knowledge may come from. Some believe that when we are in meditation, we have access to our unconscious mind, the part of ourselves that knows things instinctively. Others would say that we are linked to our higher self, which is almost like our true essence or soul. Both of these understandings are based on the belief that we have access, at core, to an incredible amount of universal knowledge, and that it is our personality that often gets in the way of us receiving this knowledge on a daily basis. When we decide to sit and meditate, we are consciously making the effort to connect with our own sources of knowledge.

Others believe that when we meditate we are able to connect with God, the universe, or any other name for the divine. Much like the traditional Judaeo–Christian understanding of prayer, meditation viewed in this way links us directly with a greater power. When we decide to meditate on something in particular, whether it is an affirmation or a picture, we are connecting with the true essence of that thing.

Likewise, when we meditate with and on a particular crystal, we are connecting with the energy and spirit of that crystal. For the purposes of this book, it doesn't matter whether you believe that you connect with the divine, your higher self, or your unconscious during meditation, because all are valid viewpoints.

Many books and teachers of meditation begin by asking us to empty or clear our mind of any thoughts or concerns. Emptying our mind is not always a particularly easy thing to do, especially if—like most people living in the modern world—we have a well-developed rational and logical mind that seems to be constantly active, giving us things to think or worry about. Instead of simply telling you to close your eyes and clear your mind of all distractions, in this section I want to teach you techniques based on ways of breathing that occupy your mind rather than silence it. This will allow for you to experience thoughts, feelings, and sensations through your nonrational or intuitive mind.

Setting time aside to meditate

When learning to meditate, it's important to set aside some time for it each day. When we assign some dedicated meditation time, we are providing our rational mind with structure, and it responds well to this. Your mind knows what is expected of it at a certain time and gradually accepts that resistance and rebellion are pointless for this short period each day. By treating your logical, rational mind like a misbehaving toddler and *not* giving in at the first sign of a tantrum, you will eventually teach it who is in charge.

Once you have assigned a set time for your daily meditation, such as first thing in the morning or last thing at night, stick to it. Whatever else is going on, always make sure that at the appointed time you are ready, sitting or lying comfortably and without distraction in your chosen meditation space.

When we say that we don't have time to meditate, what we are actually saying is that meditation is not a priority for us. What people often mean is that they don't prioritize meditation highly enough to get it done daily. I'm not saying that you are a bad person if you don't prioritize your daily meditation, but I believe that the only way to true spiritual and personal understanding is through daily, committed meditative practice. If you don't do it, you won't get it. It's up to you to decide how much of a priority spiritual and personal development is to you, and from that decision to plan your time accordingly.

Because you are reading this book, I would say that at some deep level you know that meditation is important to your life. Give yourself twenty minutes every day. That's all you need—just twenty minutes. Compared to the amount of time most of us (including me) spend watching crappy television, it's not really that much time.

Preparation

Once you are in the place where you are going to be meditating, make sure you will not be disturbed. Turn off your phone and tell anyone else who may be in the house that you don't want to be interrupted. Turning off your phone instead of just putting it on silent is important for a couple of reasons. First, we rarely, if ever, turn our phones off voluntarily. There's a part of me that is almost fearful that my world will disintegrate if my phone stops working; it's good to remind ourselves that it won't. And beyond the practical risk of alarms, vibrations, and other notifications not obeying the silence mode, I also think that knowing that your phone is turned off helps your subconscious mind to disconnect from it and the wider world it connects you to. Incidentally, I find turning off my phone and leaving it in the living room when I go to bed to be one of the most incredible aids to sleep. Initially extremely difficult, it has become a routine that allows me to truly switch off and rest for at least eight hours every twenty-four, and I highly recommend it.

Creating a safe and undisturbed meditating space is essential if you are to relax fully. It's absolutely impossible to truly calm down and leave your cares behind if even a tiny part of your mind—conscious or unconscious—is worrying whether the phone is going to ring or if someone is going to walk through the door.

Without question, the best posture for meditation and spiritual work of any kind is one where your spine is straight, because this allows for energy to flow freely and without obstruction around your body. I would say that the ideal way to sit during meditation is cross-legged on the floor, with a small cushion under your buttocks so you are not sitting directly on your folded legs. In my experience, this is the most sustainable position for any amount of time; it seems to be the most comfortable for me.

Although having your spine straight is useful and ideal, it can actually be uncomfortable, especially if you are not used to sitting up straight or have any type of physical disability. When I first started to meditate consciously, at around the age of twelve, I spent ages in a lot of pain, trying desperately to maintain a straight spine. It was twenty years later that I was finally diagnosed with a degenerative genetic disorder that effects all the systems of my body but that has most impact on my capacity to build muscle. It's not possible for me to sit still for more than three or four minutes at a time. My early attempts at meditation failed because I was so acutely aware of my physical body through the pain I was feeling that I was unable to focus on anything else.

The point of a meditation posture is to get the body into a position where it is easily forgotten. If it is uncomfortable or painful to sit upright with your spine straight, don't do it. Recognize that it might not ever be possible for you; and that's okay. Get yourself into a position that gives you as little awareness of your physical body as possible; preferably, it should be sitting instead of lying to resist the temptation to drift off to sleep, but if you have to lie down, that's fine, too.

Getting started

So, now that you are sitting (or lying) comfortably in your quiet, private space without potential distractions, you can start the actual process of meditation. If you want to burn some incense, light a candle, or play some relaxing soft music, by all means do so, but it's not compulsory.

The first part of any meditation is relaxation. Many people are never fully relaxed, even when asleep, so you should always start by becoming aware of what it is to be totally relaxed. Begin by closing your eyes and taking a deep breath. By a deep breath, I mean a breath through your nose that fills your whole body, starting at your stomach. Keep taking in air until your stomach and chest are both fully expanded, almost like a balloon. At the point where you feel you cannot physically take in any more air, hold your breath for a few seconds. I always count to three in my head to judge this. Then gently let the air out slowly through your nose until you feel there is absolutely no air left in your lungs.

This process of inhalation (breathing in) and exhalation (breathing out) is called a full breath. From here on in, whenever I say "take three full breaths," I mean three full cycles of breathing in, holding for a few seconds, and then breathing out.

Once you have taken a couple of these deep, full breaths, focus your attention on your feet. Clench your feet as tightly as you can, hold for a second, and then relax them. Then do the same for the muscles in your lower legs, clenching them as tightly as possible, holding to feel the tightness and then releasing. Move on up through your body doing this, tightening and then relaxing your thighs, buttocks, and the muscles of your lower and upper back and shoulders, making sure that every muscle in your body has been tightened and then released. As you do this, you will realize just how much tension you hold in your body.

When each muscle is released, it will be much more relaxed, so by the time you move up to your jaw, you will be sitting or lying slumped and relaxed. It's particularly important to focus on the muscles in your face, because so much tension is held here that it can sometimes be difficult to release it. When you get to your head, clench your jaw really tightly and release it. Screw your face up as much as you can, hold, and release. Then just screw your eyes up, hold, and release. Even your tongue can be relaxed; tighten the muscles in your mouth as best you can, hold, and then relax. I always find it amazing just how much stress I hold in my face.

Now that you are as physically relaxed as possible, focus your attention back to your breathing. Breathe in deeply through your nose as before. This time, I want you to feel where the breath is in your body. Physically sense the air entering your nostrils; feel the coldness of the air passing through your nose, down your throat, and into your lungs. Feel it hit the pit of your stomach and then fill up your lungs. Holding it there for a count of three, release it through your nose, feeling it leave your body bit by bit. Once you come out of your meditation—by opening your eyes and returning to full waking consciousness—you will be surprised at how deeply relaxed and "away" you will be.

The first couple of times you meditate, go through this process of following and being conscious of your breathing. When you start to follow the guided meditations in Part Four, you will have had some practice of entering into an altered state of consciousness. Even so, before each meditation I would recommend spending time going through the physical relaxation exercise described above. It's something I do almost every day.

So now, having experienced basic, simple meditation, you can move on to following the guided meditations. This form of meditation is actually significantly easier to master than the type you have practiced in this section, because you are being led through the meditation and your conscious mind is fully occupied and distracted. You will find it easy and deeply relaxing. So, become comfortable with the basic formula of meditation and move on toward meditating with the crystals.

Part Four

The Crystal Meditations

The Base Chakra

○ *Crystal* ○
BLACK OBSIDIAN

Set aside a particular time to practice this meditation when you know you will not be disturbed. Get comfortable and make sure that the room in which you are going to be meditating is warm enough. Prop yourself up on cushions, if necessary, or sit in a chair that supports your body. Select the crystal you are going to be meditating with, in this case black obsidian, and hold it gently in whichever hand feels most comfortable. You are now ready to begin.

GUIDED MEDITATION

The obsidian lake

Once you are sitting comfortably, with your eyes closed, take a long, deep breath in through your nose. Let the air you breathe in flow right to the bottom of your stomach, filling your body to the top of your chest. Hold this in-breath for a count of three, then exhale slowly and steadily, again through your nose, emptying your chest of all the air it holds. Once there is no more breath in your body, hold for another count of three. Follow this pattern of breathing twice more and notice how relaxed and at ease you feel.

With your eyes still closed, feel how supported you are where you are sitting or lying. You notice that you are sitting on a wooden chair in a dense forest of tall trees. You look down at your feet and see that they are resting on a bed of thick, cool, soft moss. You feel the texture of the moss between your bare toes and smell the damp fragrance of the forest. Notice how safe and protected you feel, and how peaceful and calm the forest is around you. As you look around, you see the trees covered in green climbing plants and hear birds singing gently. You decide to stand up, and as you begin to walk through the forest you notice that there is a clearing a little farther ahead, and you decide to make your way toward it. Take some time here to experience your journey through the forest, savoring the fresh clean smells and the peaceful sounds made by the birds and small animals that live here.

As you near the clearing, you see that in the center lies a glassy lake. You notice how the surface of this lake looks like a glossy sheet of black glass, and you see how perfectly flat and still it is until an insect or plant disturbs it, creating ripples that soon disappear. The surface of the lake is so smooth, in fact, that it is like a mirror, and as you approach the edge, you peer into the water to catch a glimpse of your reflection.

You dip your finger into the lake and feel how warm and soft the water is. You experience a strong desire to walk into it, and slowly, inch by inch, you immerse yourself in the healing warm waters—first your feet, then your ankles. As you walk into the lake up to your thighs, you realize how each part of your body becomes weightless in the water and feels almost as if it is no longer attached to the rest of you. You feel more and more at ease and relaxed as all the tension of holding your body together is dissolved and you slowly immerse yourself fully into the lake.

Take some time here to really experience the feeling of weightlessness that being in the lake gives you. Stay here for as long as you need to or want to, soaking up the healing properties of the obsidian lake. Make a mental note of any sensations you feel and in which parts of your body you feel them. Note any feelings or emotions that surface during your time in the lake, acknowledging them, thanking them for being with you, and letting them go. Once you feel you have spent enough time in the lake, slowly walk back out of it. Notice how each part of your body becomes weighted again as it leaves the water, so that when you are fully out you are aware of your whole body. Be aware, however, of how much lighter you feel generally, almost as if the physical and emotional stresses that were weighing you down before you entered the lake have been lifted from you and dissolved in the healing waters. Recognize this process as a cleansing of all the old negative feelings you had about yourself and of any blocks you may have had to real, powerful self-healing.

Now that you have come out of the lake, you are a changed person, someone ready and prepared to transform their life and begin the process of healing. Take some time here to really appreciate how good it feels to have made such an important change before you walk slowly back through the forest.

As you approach the seat on the bed of moss, you take one last look at the forest around you and know that you can come back to this place whenever you want or need to. This is your safe space. Take a seat and close your eyes again, as you slowly bring your consciousness back to your breathing. Take a deep breath in through your nose, feeling it reach the pit of your stomach and fill your chest, and hold it there for a count of three. Release this breath through your nose and make sure that every last bit of air is expelled from your body before holding for another count of three. On the second in-breath, slowly bring your attention back to the support beneath you and, when you're ready, slowly open your eyes.

The healing properties of black obsidian

PHYSICAL PROPERTIES

Black obsidian is a form of volcanic glass formed when molten lava from deep beneath the earth's surface erupts and mixes with the other minerals on the surface, melting them. It cools quickly and the result is a deep black, glossy, brittle volcanic glass. Obsidian is a deeply purifying and warming crystal; it works to relieve pain and inflammation from joints, helps with poor circulation, and aids digestion and the removal and processing of physical toxins.

EMOTIONAL AND MENTAL PROPERTIES

Obsidian is primarily a purifying and grounding crystal. This means that it has a calming, centering, and stabilizing effect on the physical body and the emotions, encouraging strength and steadfastness. It works to clean our energy of negativity, fear, anger, anxiety, and lethargy. Obsidian channels negative emotional energy held within the body out into the earth through the chakras on the soles of the feet. It makes the will strong and increases self-belief. It can be a great crystal when entering a situation of conflict, because it encourages you to feel strong and confident.

SPIRITUAL PROPERTIES

Obsidian is an essential crystal for those who want to develop themselves spiritually, because it works to clear negative energy. Used for thousands of years as a scrying tool, obsidian reflects back to us our shadow side; the parts of ourselves that we like to keep hidden; the negative personality traits; our fears, anxieties, and tender spots. It allows for us to work on them. Obsidian strengthens our roots and stabilizes us, allowing for great upward progress to be made in a relatively short space of time, but it does this by shining a light on the work we need to do. Working with obsidian then, is not easy.

Other crystals that work on the base chakra

GARNET

Garnet is a stone of abundance and prosperity. It encourages us to appreciate all the great things we experience in our daily lives. Like hematite and most grounding crystals, garnet helps to remove negative emotional energy from the body; in this way, it is a great stone to meditate with and carry when feeling down and can even be helpful for clinical depression. Garnet balances and regulates our sexual energy, so it is a great crystal to work with in dealing with any problems surrounding our sexuality. It is, therefore, also of great help for anyone dealing with the emotional effects of sexual abuse.

BOJI STONES

These strange-looking crystals—always bought in pairs of one male and one female—are fantastic grounders and balancers of energy. They encourage the flow of energy around the body, making it easier during a healing session for any energy blockages to be dissolved. The way bojis clear energetic blockages depends upon where the blockage lies, so if the root of a problem lies in the form of an old negative emotion, the crystals will make us abundantly aware of this outdated, redundant feeling so that we can consciously choose to clear it.

In a boji pair, a rough male and a smooth female stone work together to balance male and female energies. I could spend a long while talking about the various (huge) problems with gender energy. In the Western esoteric tradition (and others), the binary of male and female seems to be at the core of teachings. But really this way of understanding the world—as binary—is really only dominant since the time of Pythagoras. And it is not a helpful or particularly accurate model of the universe. Not least of all, relying on a categorization of the world based on the Pythagorean table of opposites—where male is opposite female, light is opposite dark, right opposite wrong, etc.—supports structural oppressions that are very much dominant today. I won't use the terms "male" or "female" energies in my work, and I encourage you to read about them and reconsider their use, too.

HEMATITE

Hematite gets its name from the Greek word for "blood." Unsurprisingly, hematite is primarily a crystal for the blood. It encourages the absorption of iron into the bloodstream, so it is of great use for people with menstrual cycles. Hematite also encourages the production of new blood cells, and through this process improves the supply of oxygen to the body. In part through these physically grounding properties, hematite also acts on the emotional and spiritual bodies to ground, center, and anchor.

The Sacral Chakra

○ *Crystal* ○
CARNELIAN

Set aside a particular time to practice this meditation when you know you will not be disturbed. Get comfortable and make sure that the room in which you are going to be meditating is warm enough. Prop yourself up on cushions, if necessary, or sit in a chair that supports your body. Select the crystal you are going to be meditating with, in this case carnelian, and hold it gently in whichever hand feels most comfortable. You are now ready to begin.

GUIDED MEDITATION

The carnelian fire

Once you are sitting comfortably, with your eyes closed, take a long, deep breath in through your nose. Let the air you breathe in flow right to the bottom of your stomach, filling your body up to the top of your chest. Hold this in-breath for a count of three, then exhale slowly and steadily, again through your nose, emptying your chest of all the air it holds. Once there is no more breath in your body, hold for another count of three. Follow this pattern of breathing twice more and notice how relaxed and at ease you feel.

With your eyes still closed, feel how supported you are where you are sitting or lying. You notice that your bare feet are touching dry, sandy ground. As you look around, you see that you are standing in the middle of a large desert and are surrounded by orangey-yellow sand. You feel calm and at peace here. In the distance, you see a light flickering and, although it is daylight and the sun is shining brightly, this light stands out.

You decide to move toward this light and walk slowly across the warm sand in its direction. Take a moment here to feel the hot sun on your face and soft but gritty sand between your toes as you make your way across the desert. As you come closer to the source of the light, you see that it is, in fact, a fire in the center of a large stone circle. The circle is made up of round stones just about the right size for you to carry comfortably in your hands, and one much larger stone, which you decide to sit down on. These stones, like the stone you are sitting on, are lumps of the crystal carnelian, and they appear shiny and iridescent.

Once you are seated on the largest stone, you can clearly see the fire burning in front of you in the middle of this stone circle. You take a moment now to notice how large or small this fire is, and what colors the flames are. It may be an incredibly large and bright fire, or it may barely be alight at all. Make a mental note of the state of this fire.

You pick up one of the large carnelian stones next to you and rest it on your lap. With your hands on top of this crystal, you ask it to show you what you need to be doing in your life. What should you be doing in order for the fire in front of you to either reduce in size if it is burning too fiercely or increase in heat if it is barely alight? Take some time here to receive any suggestions from the crystal. These could be things such as spending more time on your own or less time with a certain person; or perhaps taking up a hobby or spending more time developing your own ideas and confidence. Allow yourself time here to soak up any information you need from the crystal, and know that this information may come in any form. It may be that you simply get a strong sense that you need to be eating a particular type of food or eating less of something; you may receive the information in the form of words, visions, or sensations. Accept anything you receive, even if, at this time, you don't fully understand the significance.

Once you feel the information conveyed by the carnelian has come to an end, you thank the crystal for what it has shared with you and put it back in its place in the stone circle. You realize that it is now time to leave the stone circle and the fire burning inside it, but you also know that you can return to this place at any time in the future if you feel the need. You walk back the way you came, across the warm, dusty desert, and arrive back at the spot where your journey began. You close your eyes and focus on your breathing.

Take a deep breath in through your nose, feeling it reach the pit of your stomach and fill your chest, and hold it there for a count of three. Release this breath through your nose, making sure that every last bit of air is expelled from your body before holding for another count of three. On the second in-breath, slowly bring your attention back to the support beneath you and, when you're ready, slowly open your eyes.

The healing properties of carnelian

PHYSICAL PROPERTIES

Carnelian has the ability to assist your body to absorb vitamins and minerals that are essential to keep you healthy. When you are rundown or tired, carnelian is a great crystal to keep around you, because its vibration helps the body regain its natural strength and vitality. Carnelian also stimulates the metabolism and aids the digestive process, and, when we meditate with it, it can let us know which food types our body doesn't process as easily. For these reasons, carnelian is a useful stone to work with when treating physical problems such as eating disorders.

For many thousands of years, carnelian has been described and utilized as a crystal of strength—both physical and mental. Carnelian gives courage, strength, and self-belief, and its vibration can help break the cycle of physical addictions, because the root cause of such behavior is often fear and anxiety of some kind, which themselves have roots in trauma.

Carnelian has long been associated with the reduction of pain, and it has certainly been my experience that it has the ability to draw pain and tension out of the body. It is most successful at reducing pain that has its roots in fear or anxiety, and so meditating with this crystal can, therefore, ease muscular tension, irritable bowel syndrome cramping, and any nervous affliction.

EMOTIONAL AND MENTAL PROPERTIES

As we have seen, the vibration of carnelian instills courage and strength on an emotional level. It makes us feel good about ourselves and forces us to recognize our high self-value. Carnelian pushes us to make the most of our personal creativity and inspires us with the desire to paint, write, and sing. It helps us to see and understand where we are going wrong in our lives, bringing to the surface—for us to acknowledge and work through—particular emotional patterns that are not positive for us and hinder our growth. Very often, those drawn to carnelian need its stabilizing effect on the emotions.

SPIRITUAL PROPERTIES

Carnelian helps us on our spiritual path by showing us potential pitfalls. It illustrates to us what we need to do and change in our lives in order to achieve all that we are able to and reach our potential. Carnelian is the stone of the spiritual warrior; it supports us and gives us courage when we are consciously working through our issues and blockages to arrive at a state of spiritual enlightenment.

Other crystals that work on the sacral chakra

TIGER'S EYE

This crystal has been used by many different cultures over thousands of years to protect against negativity. It has the ability to strengthen the sacral chakra so that attachment to others—through either conscious or unconscious means—is unnecessary, protecting the wearer from codependent relationships. Often, when we find ourselves energetically linked to another person, it's possible to trace the instigation of this relationship back to some form of lack in ourselves: a lack of energy, willpower, or self-belief. The energy of tiger's eye balances the sacral chakra so that there is no lack and, therefore, no need to fill this space with someone else's energy.

Tiger's eye encourages self-examination. It teaches us that to get to the root of a problem we may be encountering in our lives, we need to explore what it is within ourselves that is missing or in need of attention. The energy of tiger's eye works to strengthen the part of us that may fear confronting the demons that lurk within.

CITRINE

Citrine is a strengthening stone for the physical body, and it performs this function through detoxification. The vibration of citrine cleans out any physical, emotional, and mental toxins from the body; it supports the work of the liver and kidneys, and it encourages all forms of physical elimination. Because it cleans the system of any negativity, it has a positive emotional effect, making the wearer feel happier, brighter, and generally more secure. It has long been associated with gold and wealth, partly because of its color but also because its vibration clears the path for riches and money to enter your life.

SUNSTONE

Sunstone radiates a bright, happy, and energizing light, and it encourages us to see the good in all situations. It helps us to connect with our own inner source of light and can be especially helpful in reigniting the light at the end of the tunnel that occasionally goes out.

Like all sacral chakra crystals, sunstone helps us to release any blockages we may be holding onto regarding our personal creativity, and it encourages us to disconnect energetically from negative people and experiences. It is a crystal of immense energy and power, and it is fantastic to have around when we feel lethargic, apathetic, or just gloomy.

"Sunstone radiates a bright, happy, and energizing light . . ."

The Solar Plexus Chakra

○ *Crystal* ○
YELLOW JASPER

Set aside a particular time to practice this meditation when you know you will not be disturbed. Get comfortable and make sure that the room in which you are going to be meditating is warm enough. Prop yourself up on cushions, if necessary, or sit in a chair that supports your body. Select the crystal you are going to be meditating with, in this case yellow jasper, and hold it gently in whichever hand feels most comfortable. You are now ready to begin.

GUIDED MEDITATION

The jasper sun

Once you are sitting comfortably with your eyes closed, take a long, deep breath in through your nose. Let the air you breathe in flow right to the bottom of your stomach, filling your body up to the top of your chest. Hold this in-breath for a count of three, then exhale slowly and steadily, again through your nose, emptying your chest of all the air it holds. Once there is no more breath in your body, hold for another count of three. Follow this pattern of breathing twice more and notice how relaxed and at ease you feel.

Be aware of how supported you are where you are sitting or lying. As you look down at your feet, you notice that you are standing outside the gates belonging to a beautiful house. This building may be old or it may be brand new, but what makes it distinctive is its beauty. As you gaze upon this house, you know that it is your house, and you also know that only you have access to this place. You can feel the strong, bright sunshine beating down upon your face, and you look up to see the sun shining exactly like the bright, radiant piece of jasper you have in your hand. You know that the light you feel on your body is the beautiful, healing vibrations of the jasper crystal, and you proceed toward the gates feeling peaceful and safe.

The gates to the house are closed and you take a moment to notice how they are sealed—is it a simple old-fashioned lock and key or a much more modern fingerprint-recognition system? Whatever the entry system, you notice how you hold the key, password, or fingerprint that allows for entry, and you use it to make the gates swing open.

As you walk through the beautiful gates, they close behind you and you make your way up toward the house. You decide to take a moment here and carefully observe the outside of your house. What does it look like? Are there any plants growing up the side of the building? How is the garden kept? Is it carefully ordered and maintained or wild and free? While you take a look at your house, you again notice how warm and cozy you feel with the bright sunlight on your face. Everything you see seems to have a slight tinge of yellow to it as you look through the jasper-infused sunlight.

You walk up to the front door and open it with a key you find in your pocket. As you step inside, you see in front of you another door at the end of a short corridor. You take a moment to notice anything special about this door. Is it large or small? Does it have any distinguishing features? After you've had a good look, you open the door and step inside, closing it behind you.

The first thing that strikes you as you step into the room is the powerful sense of light and warmth. There are three large windows that let in the bright yellow light and warm the room nicely. This is your room. Inside here, as you look around, you notice all of the things that make you feel the safest you have ever felt. There may be particular photos, childhood toys, favorite books—anything that makes you feel protected, safe, and secure. The floor is carpeted in the most beautiful bright yellow, and in one of the corners is a large couch, almost like a daybed, filled with the greatest number of pillows and cushions you have ever seen. As you slip your shoes off and walk with bare feet across the deep, soft, carpeted floor, you decide to snuggle up on the couch.

This room and its contents—including the soft, welcoming, and comfortable couch with its pillows and cushions—is your safe place. In here, you are protected from everything and anything—no one and nothing can reach you here unless you choose to let them—and you feel calm, safe, and more relaxed than ever before.

You begin to notice how any tension, anxiety, fear, or concerns you may have had before stepping into the room have totally left you. You recognize that, in this room, fear and anxiety simply do not exist, and you can feel your solar plexus chakra relax completely—possibly for the first time in a long while—because you are so totally protected and safe.

You think about how you felt before you entered your safe place. If you were aware of being particularly sensitive to other people's energy and moods, you notice how spending time in this environment let your usually overly open solar plexus close down a little. This means you are not bombarded by feelings that are not yours or are in no way helpful to you. If you felt that your solar plexus was closed—that you had difficulty connecting to how you felt about situations, or that you were unsure about trusting your own judgment—you now notice that spending time in your safe place lets your solar plexus open up and reconnect to the rest of your being. This isn't something you have to try to do—it will have already happened naturally.

Once you feel you have spent as long as you need or want to in your safe place with the bright jasper light shining down on you, calming and balancing your solar plexus, you step off the couch and walk back across the deep soft carpet, feeling the texture between your bare toes as you head toward your shoes and the door. After slipping your shoes back on, you open the door and step through, closing it behind you. As you find yourself back in the corridor and make your way toward the front door of your house—opening it, stepping through, and closing it behind you—you notice how dramatically different you feel.

Any fear or anxiety, feelings of disconnection from, or mistrust of, your personal judgment have completely gone. You feel refreshed, happy, and calm, especially because you know you can come back to this place whenever you want to and it is particularly easy to do so when you hold your jasper crystal while meditating.

Now that you have received all the healing from the jasper crystal, you decide to come back to full consciousness. Take a deep breath in through your nose, feeling it reach the pit of your stomach and fill your chest, and hold it there for a count of three. Release this breath, again through your nose, and make sure that every last bit of air is expelled from your body before holding it for another count of three. On the second in-breath, slowly bring your attention back to the support beneath you and, when you're ready, slowly open your eyes.

The healing properties of yellow jasper

PHYSICAL PROPERTIES

Jasper, like carnelian, is a form of quartz combined with other minerals. It has the healing attributes of quartz along with the grounding properties of its other, more earthy, inclusions. Jasper is an excellent worry stone; it calms the nervous system and reassures us that everything will work out well in the end. Yellow jasper helps with the physical release of toxins and ensures that the body's energy remains stable and constant during such releases. For this reason it is an excellent crystal to carry or play with when releasing any emotions through speech, as well as when purifying the body during a detoxifying diet. It supports the digestion and is especially helpful when working on digestive disorders, an upset stomach, or a nervous stomach. It is a great crystal to work with when feeling heavy, sick, or tired, because it helps the body to flush out anything negative and unnecessary.

In my experience, it is occasionally the case that people who believe themselves to be sensitive or even allergic to particular foods, such as wheat or dairy, often have an open and active solar plexus. In such cases, working with the energy of Jasper can have a dramatic effect. Jasper is a good crystal to use when recovering from any urinary problems, such as cystitis or water retention, and in such cases works best when taken as an elixir (*see page 129*).

EMOTIONAL AND MENTAL PROPERTIES

Jasper is not just a physical detoxifier, it also clears out old and negative emotional energy, especially anything that makes us feel anxious, nervous, or physically sick. Jasper acts like a good friend offering emotional support; it encourages self-belief and dispels light depressions, anger, and mood swings. Self-doubt is reduced significantly, and the vibration of jasper also dispels any fear of others. Those who feel the need for the approval and confirmation of the people around them find jasper incredibly useful, because it strengthens belief in one's own judgment.

SPIRITUAL PROPERTIES

Yellow jasper is a deeply protective and grounding solar plexus stone, meaning that it helps our solar plexus to regulate and discern. Think of it like a companion on your spiritual journey; it is there to affirm your right choices and intuitions and protect you from those that are not in your best interests.

> *"Yellow jasper helps with the physical release of toxins . . ."*

Other crystals that work on the solar plexus

AMBER

Not technically a crystal, amber is the natural resin of a now extinct ancient pine tree that grew in northern Europe in semitropical conditions. The sap from the tree would fall to the ground, and over millions of years it ended up under the ocean. Much later, after being banged about and naturally polished, the amber was washed up on beaches all along the Baltic coast.

Crystal healers use amber today to strengthen the solar plexus as well as to protect against negative energies and the influence of others. Amber has the ability to create an energy barrier that repels and resists negativity, almost like the way plastic resists water. Amber is incredibly useful for people who find themselves dealing with difficult or aggressive individuals on a daily basis, because it prevents any of that negativity from affecting them.

YELLOW CALCITE

Acting much like yellow jasper in its ability to detoxify, yellow calcite has been used for many centuries to boost the wearer's energy levels. Because of its interesting optical properties, calcite is birefringent, meaning it has the ability to refract light twice. Calcite has, therefore, been understood to double the energy of anything associated with it. Marble is the most common form of calcite, and many temples and churches in the ancient world were constructed from this material, because it was thought to double the spiritual energy of the building. Many people believe that calcite has the ability to boost not only their vital energy but also their spiritual energy and abilities.

MOONSTONE (NOT RAINBOW)

Moonstone—but not the more spectacular rainbow moonstone—is another strong solar plexus stone. As we have learned, the solar plexus is an energy center connected with personal power and the emotions, and moonstone is the strongest of all emotional balancers. Women especially find the energy of moonstone incredibly useful, because it helps balance hormones and regulate mood swings that can sometimes accompany hormonal changes. The vibration of yellow or orange-tinged moonstone keeps the solar plexus balanced and not too open.

The Heart Chakra

○ *Crystal* ○
GREEN QUARTZ

---

*Set aside a particular time to practice this meditation
when you know you will not be disturbed. Get
comfortable and make sure that the room in which you
are going to be meditating is warm enough. Prop
yourself up on cushions, if necessary, or sit in a chair
that supports your body. Select the crystal you are going
to be meditating with, in this case green quartz, and
hold it gently in whichever hand feels most comfortable.
You are now ready to begin.*

GUIDED MEDITATION

The green quartz garden

Once you are sitting comfortably, with your eyes closed, take a long, deep breath in through your nose. Let the air you breathe in flow right to the bottom of your stomach, filling your body up to the top of your chest. Hold this in-breath for a count of three, then exhale slowly and steadily, again through your nose, emptying your chest of all the air it holds. Once there is no more breath in your body, hold for another count of three. Follow this pattern of breathing twice more and notice how relaxed and at ease you feel.

With your eyes still closed, feel how supported you are where you are sitting or lying. You look down to see that you are sitting on a wooden bench. As you take a moment to notice your surroundings, you can feel warm sunlight on your face and a gentle, cool breeze stirring your hair. You realize that you are sitting on a bench inside a garden. This garden is enclosed by tall walls built of ancient brick, and at the far end you can see the entrance gate. Pay attention to the walls and any creeping plants that may be growing on them. By looking at the walls, notice how ancient this garden must be.

You decide to get up from your bench and take a stroll around the garden. As you look around, you can see that, instead of being a large, single garden, this place actually has seven different archways and gates that lead to other, separate gardens. Each of the gardens seems to be color-coordinated so that the flowers and plants in each area focus upon one color. You notice how the overall feeling is one of complete peace and tranquility, and the strongest color of all is green, almost the exact same shade of green as the green quartz crystal in your hand.

As you wander around, you notice how you are drawn to one archway leading to a particular garden. You decide to walk toward this archway, and as you near it you can smell a strong, distinctive fragrance of roses. The archway may be low or high—notice how easy it is to enter this garden. Are there gates keeping people, including you, out? Or is the entrance to this garden fully open and unobstructed?

There may be a person guarding the entrance to this place, or even a particular memory. If so, you take notice of who that person is and may even decide to ask him or her something. Whatever you find here, you enter the garden. There may be no one obstructing the entrance to the garden—in which case, you walk straight in.

The first thing that strikes you as you enter this sacred place is the scent of roses, closely followed by the sight of hundreds of these beautiful flowers. You decide to take a moment here to notice how large this rose garden is—does it have clearly defined limits, like the walls of the first garden, or does it seem to stretch into infinity? Are the roses neatly lined up in a strict order or are they wild and free? You feel yourself being drawn toward one rose in particular, and you bend down to smell its scent and feel its soft, velvety petals gently stroke the skin of your face. As you close your eyes to concentrate all your awareness on the scent of the rose, you feel yourself falling into the flower so that all you become aware of is being completely enveloped in the essence of the rose.

It is here in this state that you become aware of someone who loves you. You may see that person; you may simply think of him or her; or that person may speak to you. What you feel here, however, is that you are completely and utterly, unconditionally loved. In this state of peace and tranquility, where nothing can harm you and only those people who have loved you can be found, you are reminded of your true essence.

When you become aware of this person, you notice that he or she has something to offer you. This gift may come in the form of a physical object, or it may be a word or a prayer. Perhaps it is simply a hug or a kiss. Whatever you are given, accept it with gratitude. You may spend as long as you like in this state of total lovedness, and when you are ready to leave, you can feel your awareness being brought back to the rose garden. You can see the other roses around you and smell their beautiful scent. You decide to leave the rose garden in the same way you entered it, walking back toward the archway. You take a moment here to notice if the entrance to the rose garden has changed at all—if there is anyone or anything restricting access to the garden, is there still a person there, or has he or she moved on? Is the height of the archway the same, or has it changed?

As you move back into the main garden, you notice again the bright-green color that seems to permeate everything. You know that you can return to this place whenever you want to, and again experience the safe, comforting feeling of being completely loved. You know it is especially easy to reconnect with this space when you meditate while holding your green quartz crystal.

Now that you have received all the healing from the green quartz crystal, you decide to come back to full consciousness. Take a deep breath in through your nose, feeling it reach the pit of your stomach and fill your chest, and hold it there for a count of three. Release this breath, again through your nose, making sure that every last bit of air is expelled from your body before holding it for another count of three. On the second in-breath, gradually bring your attention back to the support beneath you and, when you're ready, slowly open your eyes.

The healing properties of green quartz

PHYSICAL PROPERTIES

Green quartz is an excellent stone to carry with you and use when you have any form of chest infection, breathing difficulty, or cough, because it works particularly on the chest. It is also, unsurprisingly, an effective heart stone, making it especially useful for people with physical heart problems. Green quartz works with the endocrine system to keep the body's hormones balanced; the cells of endocrine organs secrete and release hormones, which are carried in the bloodstream to where they are most needed.

EMOTIONAL AND MENTAL PROPERTIES

Green quartz is a calming stone; it soothes the emotions and quells any anger. The color associated with the heart chakra, as we have seen, is green, and this green form of quartz is wonderful for soothing, calming, and comforting the heart.

Green quartz eases heartache and makes us feel loved and protected. It is a strengthening stone as well, so gradually and gently builds emotional confidence. If you have been through a tough time emotionally, green quartz will help your heart to repair itself.

The vibration of green quartz balances all energy—especially male and female energies—allowing for balanced decisions and better judgment. It also encourages and enhances decisiveness and increases leadership abilities, so if you find yourself in a situation where you need to be in control, green quartz can help.

SPIRITUAL PROPERTIES

A form of green quartz called green aventurine, which has a shimmering or glistening effect, has long been used by Native Americans to help connect with spirit guides; the stone was often held over the heart while meditating. We can use the energy of green quartz to open the heart chakra to become more aware of the love of our spirit guides. As we learned earlier (*see pages 34–36*), we can develop the top three chakras only when the heart chakra is fully open, and in this way green quartz helps spiritual development by opening, healing, and strengthening the heart chakra.

Other crystals that work on the heart chakra

ROSE QUARTZ

Rose quartz is possibly one of the most well-known healing crystals, and rightly so. Its incredibly loving energy soothes, softens, comforts, and supports the heart and the emotions. Rose quartz is the love stone. Not only does it make you feel loved when holding or wearing it, but it also encourages self-love and acceptance. Rose quartz has the reputation of being able to draw your true love to you. In order to truly love another person, you must be able to love yourself first; and by teaching you self-love, rose quartz ensures you fall in love only with someone you deserve and who will love you truly. I believe strongly that one of the most powerful things you can do to manifest true love in your life is to work with the energy of rose quartz.

Rose quartz is also associated with fertility. It is well-known that babies are more easily conceived by women who are relaxed and happy. The energy of rose quartz encourages self-love as well as the love of others, creating the perfect environment for conception to occur.

MALACHITE

Malachite is a deep forest green stone with veins of lighter green running through it. This crystal encourages positive emotional change and, for this reason, the energy of malachite can feel a little pushy and not as soft and gentle as rose quartz.

Malachite helps you to see emotional situations more clearly and clarify how you feel about certain people and events. Sometimes we resist accepting something we know to be true, although to do so would move us forward, and it is here that the energy of malachite can be helpful. Malachite is a loving stone and will push you only in a direction that is best for you. Malachite is not to be used when making gem elixirs (*see page 129*), because it is slightly water soluble.

RHODOCHROSITE

Another crystal that works specifically on the heart chakra is rhodochrosite. This crystal has a soft, gentle energy similar to rose quartz, although the energy of rhodochrosite is especially associated with the love of the mother. Maternal love is one of the strongest forms of love, and rhodochrosite makes you feel protected and loved unconditionally. It is a stone that is, unsurprisingly, excellent for pregnant women, nursing mothers, and children, as well as anyone needing nurturing and looking after. Rhodochrosite has also been used to balance the heart rate and the pulse.

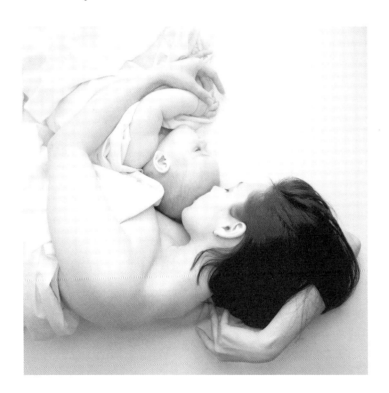

The Throat Chakra

◦ *Crystal* ◦
BLUE QUARTZ

Set aside a particular time to practice this meditation when you know you will not be disturbed. Get comfortable and make sure that the room in which you are going to be meditating is warm enough. Prop yourself up on cushions, if necessary, or sit in a chair that supports your body. Select the crystal you are going to be meditating with, in this case blue quartz, and hold it gently in whichever hand feels most comfortable. You are now ready to begin.

GUIDED MEDITATION

The blue quartz audience

Once you are sitting comfortably with your eyes closed, take a long, deep breath in through your nose. Let the air you breathe in flow right to the bottom of your stomach, filling your body up to the top of your chest. Hold this in-breath for a count of three, then exhale slowly and steadily, again through your nose, emptying your chest of all the air it holds. Once there is no more breath in your body, hold for another count of three. Follow this pattern of breathing twice more and notice how relaxed and at ease you feel.

You become aware that you are standing in what looks like the backstage area of a large theater. You can hear the sound of hushed chatter as a lot of people settle down into their seats. As you look around, you notice many people preparing busily for the performance that is about to begin. You approach one of these people but get no response from that person, and you soon realize that you are invisible. No one can see you at all. Even more significantly, you cannot be heard by anyone. It's as if you've had your voice taken away and find yourself silenced. As you make your way around this place, exploring and taking note of all you see, you decide to take a peek at the stage itself.

On the stage, you can see the back of someone standing behind the closed stage curtain. This person looks familiar to you, and you walk over to him or her, aware that you cannot be seen or heard by anyone. As you get closer to the person in the center of the stage, you realize that this person is, in fact, yourself. Just at that moment, you hear the curtains being opened and the audience in front of the stage beginning to clap.

As you look at the people in the audience, you begin to recognize a few of them. You see people you have spoken to recently, perhaps your boss, a work colleague, or friend. You also notice people you may not have seen or spoken to for many years. As you spend a while looking at these different people, you realize what they all have in common—you have something you need to tell them. It may be that you felt put down recently by your boss, or that you didn't stand up for yourself properly during a meeting with a colleague. It may even be that a friend of yours upset you and, although you said nothing about it at the time, you stewed about it later on. As you take a look at each of the people in the audience, you note what it is you needed or wanted to say to them.

As you work your way through all of the people sitting in the seats before you, you come across the front row of people. You didn't see these people when you first took a glance at the audience, but looking more closely you now realize that sitting in this front row are those people to whom you have been unable to say something for many years. Perhaps you see your parents here or an old school friend. The important thing about this row of people is either that they have prevented you from saying something or that you've felt unable to speak to them at some point in your life. By not speaking to them and voicing your feelings, you've felt held back in some way, personally, emotionally, or even professionally. Don't be surprised if you recognize people sitting here whom you haven't even thought about for many years.

Once you have identified most of the people in the audience, you become aware of a strange, strong desire to speak to them. As you move toward yourself standing on the stage, you decide to walk into your body. You take a few steps forward and feel your spirit enter your body; suddenly you become aware of being whole and complete. You open your mouth to speak and realize that, at last, sound can be heard and you can talk.

As you look at all the people in the audience, you decide to speak to each one, in turn, to tell them whatever it was that you felt unable to express in the past. Perhaps you start with seemingly insignificant situations, such as a small disagreement with a friend, looking at that person directly in the eye and opening your mouth to speak. After you have said your piece to your friend, you feel empowered, calm, and satisfied. In this space, when you are on this stage, no one has the right or ability to silence you. When you speak, people have to listen and take note. You move from one person to the next, feeling more and more empowered each time you say what you need to say. Finally, you reach the people in your front row.

You take a deep breath, noticing how the experience of expressing yourself has made you feel calm and relaxed but also confident. You know that whatever you say here will be taken seriously and will not be silenced. As you look each one of these people in the eye and say what you have been unable to express for many years, months, days, or weeks, you notice an incredible sense of something being released and lifted from your energy. Any anxiety you may have been carrying connected to speaking your truth freely is lifted and you feel liberated.

Once you have expressed your feelings to each of the people in this front row, you know your work here is done and you decide to return. You have learned just how much you can be held back by not speaking out at the time, and how this can connect you to negative emotions. You realize just how liberating and empowering speaking your mind can be and resolve to do it significantly more in your day-to-day life.

As you walk backstage, you feel calm, in control of your emotions, and happy. You know you can come back to this place whenever you feel the need and that, by connecting with the energy of the blue quartz crystal, you will feel able and willing to express yourself clearly, confidently, and with strength.

Now that you have received all the healing from the blue quartz crystal, you decide to return to full consciousness. Take a deep breath in through your nose, feeling it reach the pit of your stomach and fill your chest, and hold it there for a count of three. Release this breath, again through your nose, making sure every last bit of air is expelled from your body before holding for another count of three. On the second in-breath, slowly bring your attention back to the support beneath you and, when you're ready, slowly open your eyes.

The healing properties of blue quartz

PHYSICAL PROPERTIES

Blue quartz is one of the most cooling crystals. It is cold to the touch and doesn't store heat, so even on a hot day the crystal won't feel warm. This makes it useful during the summer, especially when trying to ease the effects of sunburn. It is also an excellent skin stone. It calms, soothes, and reduces all forms of inflammation, so it can be applied in elixir form to any rashes, burns, or blemishes. Blue quartz works particularly well on the throat, and it can ease and soothe a painful throat or a cough.

EMOTIONAL AND MENTAL PROPERTIES

Blue quartz is an emotional coolant. It calms and soothes the nerves and instills peace and a sense of serenity. One of its most interesting and useful properties is the ability to dissolve anger. When you feel yourself reaching boiling point, blue quartz can bring you down from that ridge and make you see sense in a calm and serene way. Its calming, cooling energy has an effect on the mental function as well, and it can quell any temper that may interfere with rational thinking, allowing for good decisions to be made and preventing rash or harsh judgments from being passed while in a state of hot-headedness.

SPIRITUAL PROPERTIES

Because it opens the throat chakra, the energy of blue quartz lets us express ourselves fully and truthfully. A phrase often used to describe the energy of blue quartz is "speaking one's truth." Being able to communicate in a truthful and honest way is essential to any spiritual development. The spiritual properties of blue quartz are primarily connected with encouraging and supporting this function. If you can stand up for yourself or another person and verbally express the truth as you feel it, then you are without question developing yourself spiritually.

Other crystals that work on the throat chakra

BLUE CALCITE

Blue calcite also has a cooling energy although, unlike blue quartz, it strengthens the memory. This crystal has been used for many centuries to help with the recalling of past-life experiences. It is believed that blue calcite, unlike any other color of calcite, focuses the mind and increases the brain's ability to receive and hold onto knowledge. Like blue quartz, it eases communication and encourages expression.

BLUE KYANITE

This crystal helps us to connect with the angelic realms. Working with and wearing blue kyanite will help you to communicate with your own angels and spirit guides. Blue kyanite teaches your body and your energy to communicate in a loving way, encouraging harmless communication as opposed to violent confrontation. This isn't a matter of simply avoiding swear words or curses; instead, it is about how you speak: your intonation, rate of speech, and the intention behind everything you say. The soft and gentle energy of blue kyanite teaches your energy to be the same when communicating.

TURQUOISE

A sacred stone of the Native Americans for many centuries, turquoise is a well-known healing mineral. This blue-green stone is primarily known for its use in spiritual rituals and as a memory stone to aid memory and assist in recalling past events, even past lives. Turquoise allows for the emotions and energy of the heart chakra to be fully and easily expressed through the throat chakra, and, for this reason, it is known as a bridging crystal. So strong is the link between turquoise and the expression of emotions that it is said the stone will break or dramatically change color if a partner is unfaithful.

The Brow Chakra

○ *Crystal* ○

SODALITE

Set aside a particular time to practice this meditation when you know you will not be disturbed. Get comfortable and make sure that the room in which you are going to be meditating is warm enough. Prop yourself up on cushions, if necessary, or sit in a chair that supports your body. Select the crystal you are going to be meditating with, in this case sodalite, and hold it gently in whichever hand feels most comfortable. You are now ready to begin.

GUIDED MEDITATION

The sodalite mountain

Once you are sitting comfortably with your eyes closed, take a long, deep breath in through your nose. Let the air you breathe in flow right to the bottom of your stomach, filling your body up to the top of your chest. Hold this in-breath for a count of three, then exhale slowly and steadily, again through your nose, emptying your chest of all the air it holds. Once there is no more breath in your body, hold for another count of three. Follow this pattern of breathing twice more and notice how relaxed and at ease you feel.

As you look down at your feet, you notice that you are standing in a forest with many trees all around you. In front of you is what appears to be a large stone or rock formation. As you move toward it through the trees, you begin to realize just how enormous this structure must be. You recognize that you are, in fact, standing at the foot of an incredibly high mountain. As you look up, you are aware that you cannot see the summit from where you are standing.

Unlike any other mountain you have seen before, this is made up entirely of a deep blue stone—it is a sodalite mountain. As you walk around the bottom of the mountain, you notice deep, wide steps that seem to wind their way up the mountain, slightly hidden by the undergrowth. You decide to climb these steps. Take a moment here to notice how you feel as you climb: is it easy and fun to do, or are you slightly breathless and needing a lot of little breaks?

As you climb higher and higher, you are aware that the scenery around you changes slightly. You begin to catch glimpses of branches and leaves instead of just tree trunks, and as you climb higher still, you start to notice brightly colored birds flying around you. You know that you can stop at any point on this long journey upward and feel no panic or pressure to continue; but, with each step you take, you notice something new and exciting, and this makes you want to keep going.

Eventually, after what seems like hours of climbing, you reach a point where you can see beyond the tops of the trees. This is an amazing stage in your journey, and you stop for a moment to take a look at the scenery around you. Notice what you can see here. Are there any particular sounds or smells? Although you can see the tops of the trees, a thick layer of cloud prevents you from glimpsing much more; and because you can see that the mountain reaches farther and farther into these clouds, you decide to continue your journey.

As you make your way through the thick layer of cloud, you feel the water vapor enter your lungs. Soon you realize that you breathe more easily with each breath you take, and that you are becoming almost light-headed. As you are walking through these clouds, you can see only a little way ahead, and you notice how you are relying more and more on trust on where to place your next step. Each time you put your foot down, your trust is rewarded with a safe footing, and you learn that your physical eyes are not as necessary for navigation as you once thought.

Finally, you begin to feel the clouds thinning, and eventually you reach the top of the mountain. As you pull yourself up to the summit and catch your breath, you take a look around and are truly amazed. Beyond the treetops that now seem so far below, you see an entire world you didn't even know existed. Other mountains rise out of a sea of greenery, waterfalls gush and roar in the distance, and far away on the horizon you see the silvery blue shimmer of the ocean. You are even more surprised and delighted by the number of different energies and beings that reside in these high altitudes, and which you can now see.

Fairies fly past you; different swathes of color drift by like sheets being pulled through the wind. The visions you now see are those you have longed to experience but were unable to do so previously. From this great height, your problems seem small and insignificant. You have been given the gift of higher vision and greater perspective, and it is a gift that can never be taken back. You know that whenever you feel the need, or you simply want to experience this feeling of immense vision again, you can return to the sodalite mountain. As you take your last glimpse of this usually hidden world, you descend from the mountain summit and make your way back down.

You carefully retrace your steps through the thick layer of cloud, remembering how it was that, by trusting your feelings, you were able to reach the summit in the first place. You walk down the mountain carefully but quickly and arrive at the bottom. It seems like a long while since you began your ascent. Here, you take a moment to recall where the steps begin that lead to the top so that you can always return to them, and you make your way back through the trees to where you began your journey.

Now that you have received all the healing from the sodalite mountain, you decide to come back to full consciousness. Take a deep breath in through your nose, feeling it reach the pit of your stomach and fill your chest, and hold it there for a count of three. Release this breath, again through your nose, and make sure that every last bit of air is expelled from your body before holding for another count of three. On the second in-breath, slowly bring your attention back to the support beneath you and, when you're ready, slowly open your eyes.

The healing properties of sodalite

PHYSICAL PROPERTIES

This crystal alleviates headaches caused by a buildup of mental energy. It reduces stress and tension by ordering thoughts in the mind. Sodalite has been used to increase the body's metabolism and works well to reduce discomfort associated with digestive disorders. It can also be useful for people who experience insomnia, primarily by reducing stress and allowing for the subconscious mind to rest. Some people use soda-lite to help the body absorb calcium.

EMOTIONAL AND MENTAL PROPERTIES

Sodalite creates a state of calmness and tranquility. It helps us to feel as if we belong and reduces the need to look for approval and confirmation from others. Through its calming and stress-relieving actions, sodalite silences the internal chatter of self-doubt and lack of confidence, and it allows for the emotional body to remember its natural state of power and self-confidence. Because sodalite is a great crystal for ordering the thoughts, it can be useful when you need to remember a large amount of information in a particular order. This crystal builds your confidence in your mental and intellectual abilities, primarily by silencing internal chatter and encouraging rational thinking.

SPIRITUAL PROPERTIES

Sodalite works primarily on the brow chakra to clear away any self-doubt and self-criticism when it comes to seeing beyond the physical. Its stress-relieving properties quieten the mind so that psychic occurrences and other energies beyond those of normal day-to-day life can be experienced. Often, psychic messages are lost in the constant babble of the unconscious mind. Sodalite works to order and quell this chatter, thus allowing for psychic energies to be identified.

Other crystals that work on the brow chakra

LAPIS LAZULI

This crystal has been used for many thousands of years as a stone of clairvoyance. It can significantly enhance the ability to receive and, more important, to understand visions and pictures beyond the physical. Lapis lazuli also works well on the energy of the throat chakra and, for this reason, it is helpful in expressing whatever is seen. Often, people with an ability to see things psychically have a problem communicating what they see to others through fear of either getting it wrong or describing it poorly. Lapis lazuli can help. As one of the oldest-known minerals, it can give the wearer access to ancient knowledge.

RAINBOW MOONSTONE

Unlike its sister, moonstone, this crystal has bands of rainbows running through it. Rainbow moonstone is a fantastic dream stone; it can be used to help you remember your dreams and to dream in full color. Like plain moonstone, rainbow moonstone balances the emotions, and the rainbow version utilizes this property to allow for clear, unbiased understandings to be gained while meditating.

LABRADORITE

The main function of this stone is to help you assimilate the information gained from your intuition into your daily life. Labradorite helps your logical and intuitive minds work together to give you the most information possible. This crystal also has aura-cleansing properties, and wearing it ensures your energy remains clean and bright. Labradorite shimmers with different layers of feldspar and is, in fact, closely related to rainbow moonstone. Both crystals enhance psychic abilities.

The Crown Chakra

∘ *Crystal* ∘
CLEAR QUARTZ

Set aside a particular time to practice this meditation when you know you will not be disturbed. Get comfortable and make sure that the room in which you are going to be meditating is warm enough. Prop yourself up on cushions, if necessary, or sit in a chair that supports your body. Select the crystal you are going to be meditating with, in this case clear quartz, and hold it gently in whichever hand feels most comfortable. You are now ready to begin.

GUIDED MEDITATION

The crystal chamber of knowledge

Once you are sitting comfortably with your eyes closed, take a long, deep breath in through your nose. Let the air you breathe in flow right to the bottom of your stomach, filling your body up to the top of your chest. Hold this in-breath for a count of three, then exhale slowly and steadily, again through your nose, emptying your chest of all the air it holds. Once there is no more breath in your body, hold for another count of three. Follow this pattern of breathing twice more and notice how relaxed and at ease you feel.

Become aware of the point at the top of your head. As you concentrate on this point, notice how all your awareness drains from every other part of your body and is focused here. Imagine that every bit of your soul and spirit is now centered in this tiny point. Visualize your spirit as a tiny light leaving your physical body through this spot on your head, flying toward the crystal in your hand.

Take a moment to appreciate how good it feels to be free from the constraints of your physicality. Notice how calm and at peace you feel, knowing that you can return to your body at any point. As you move toward the crystal in your hand, you feel yourself entering the stone.

As you enter the crystal, you take a moment to look around you. You find yourself in a long corridor with many doors leading off in different directions. The walls and floor of this crystal are smooth and glassy—notice what color they are and how they feel to the touch. Are they warm or cold? Are they transparent and filled with light or are they solid in color?

As you move down the corridor, you feel yourself being drawn toward a particular door. You approach it, making a note of how the door looks. Is there any hardware on the door—perhaps a knocker, handle, or keyhole? As you take a look at the door, you notice a plaque above it that reads "Chamber of Knowledge." You gently turn the handle or push the door open and step through into the room beyond.

Take a moment to really look at this space. What is in here? You have stepped into the crystal's Chamber of Knowledge—how is this knowledge contained? Are there rows and rows of bookcases filled with thousands of books? Or are there computers holding all the information this crystal contains? There may be neither of these things in this room, because each crystal is unique. Spend a moment here to look around completely and sense how you feel.

As you take a look around this Chamber of Knowledge, you notice a large table in the center of the room. You also notice a small staircase on the far right-hand side of the room, leading upward to what looks like a room beyond. You decide to walk over to the staircase and climb the stairs to the upper floor.

At the top of the stairs there is a door, and you turn the handle and walk through into the room beyond. In front of you, you immediately see a small table and chair. There is a clear glass on the table. This glass seems to be filled with some form of clear liquid, although it is shining so much and so brightly that it looks almost like it is filled with liquid light. You have an overwhelming desire to drink this liquid and, as you pick up the glass, you know that this is the pure healing energy of clear quartz in liquid form. You drink the liquid and feel the cool, bright, soothing energy flow down your throat into your body, filling every cell with light and peace. It feels wonderful to take this energy of the clear quartz into your body, and you feel cleansed, healed, and illuminated from within.

As you finish your glass of clear quartz elixir and place it back on the table, you notice how it magically refills itself. If you want to, you can drink another glass of the liquid so that you feel even brighter, cleaner, and more healed. Once you have taken your fill of the clear quartz healing, you decide to open the door and walk back down the stairs, back into the Chamber of Knowledge. You notice that the table in the room now has a box on it. As you walk over to the table, you see that this box has your name on it, and you know that inside is a gift for you from the crystal.

You lift the lid of the box and see what the crystal has given you. This gift may be a physical object or it may be a sound, a vibration, or a color. It may even be a memory of something or a scent. Whatever this gift is, do not reject it or think that what you see is somehow wrong. Don't try to think too much about what you receive, either.

As you take a final look around this Chamber of Knowledge, you know that you can return here whenever you want to receive information contained in the crystal or to drink the healing liquid in the room above. You make your way back toward the door through which you entered, open it, and step through, closing it behind you.

You find yourself in the corridor again, and you walk back along it to the entrance to the crystal. You leave the crystal in the same way as you entered it and, as a tiny point of light, you fly out of the crystal and back into your physical body, entering it at the same point.

As you become aware of being back in physical form, you take some deep breaths to fully integrate your spirit and body. You may want to wiggle your toes or stretch your arms as you become gradually more aware of your physicality again. Take a deep breath in through your nose, feeling it reach the pit of your stomach and fill your chest, and hold it there for a count of three. Releasing this breath, again through your nose, make sure every last bit of air is expelled from your body before holding it for another count of three. On the second in-breath, slowly bring your attention back to the support beneath you and, when you're ready, slowly open your eyes.

The healing properties of clear quartz

PHYSICAL PROPERTIES

Known as the master healer, clear quartz has the ability to heal and alleviate any illness and make you generally much healthier. Its pure and clean vibration clears out old, toxic energy; if you are feeling run-down or ill, clear quartz will improve your situation. This is an excellent crystal to work with if you have any vision problems, because it helps you see things much more clearly, both emotionally and physically.

EMOTIONAL AND MENTAL PROPERTIES

Clear quartz works to bring clarity of vision and understanding. If you are concerned that you might not be getting the whole picture in a certain situation, working with clear quartz will assist you. This crystal also helps you clarify how you feel about specific people and situations. Work with it if there is a sense of emotional confusion anywhere in your life, but be prepared for things to be made especially clear to you.

Clear quartz encourages clarity of thinking and decisive action. Unlike most healing stones, it stimulates the rational and logical mind as much as the psychic and intuitive one. It brings you confidence. Most interesting and helpful of all is its ability to store programming better than any other crystal, so if you need help with something—for example, remembering data or being more assertive—you can program the crystal to assist you (*see pages 54–55*). It will hold this programming clearly and help you in the required way for as long as you have it near to you.

SPIRITUAL PROPERTIES

Clear quartz is perhaps best known as the stone of psychic development, because it opens and activates the crown chakra. Its pure vibration clears the path between your rational mind and the universe, allowing for and supporting good communication between your spirit guides and yourself. Meditating with clear quartz, and working with it regularly once you have worked through each of your chakras separately, will ensure a clear channel is established and that all your chakras remain clear.

Other crystals that work on the crown chakra

AMETHYST

This crystal is great at reducing stress, because it acts like a sponge for negative energy, making an environment (whether a room, person, or house) feel calmer and less negative. It alleviates headaches caused by a buildup of energy—especially anxiety—and generally calms the nerves. Its ability to reduce stress and anxiety allows for meditation to become easier, so it is an excellent stone to work with when first learning to meditate. Its name comes from the Greek *amethustos* ("sober"), referring to the crystal's ability to prevent intoxication from alcohol.

SELENITE

Selenite is one of the most calming and peaceful of all the healing crystals. It has the ability to silence even the most chattering mind and bring great relief from tension, especially tension focused around the head. For this reason, it can help with insomnia. It can be a useful stone to carry during pregnancy, because it balances the emotions and brings peace, and this will, in turn, affect the baby in a positive way.

CELESTITE

Celestite gets its name from the Latin for "heavens," and this crystal is especially good at helping us to connect with our angels and the celestial beings. Its energy is calming and peaceful, like most crown chakra stones, and it helps us to understand and hear the communications of the higher realms and to communicate in life in a more angelic way.

PART FIVE

Going Farther

The chakra healing layout

This basic crystal healing layout has been used all over the world for many hundreds, perhaps thousands, of years. As we have learned, each crystal in our set has an affinity with a particular chakra, or energy center. In this layout, we will be placing these crystals on another person on their corresponding chakras to activate them, and then leaving them for a set period of time to do their work.

Choosing the right environment

Before embarking on any healing work, it is essential to choose an appropriate space. Much as with meditation, it is important that the place in which you choose to perform your healing is quiet, has a door that can be securely closed, and is warm. The intention is to create a space that feels safe, calm, comfortable, and protected. Laying the person you're helping to heal on the kitchen table while the rest of the family walks in and out just isn't going to work.

The ideal space to perform healing is a room dedicated to spiritual practice. However, few people have the luxury of such a space, and so anywhere quiet and comfortable that can be shut off from the outside world will do. If you don't have a therapy couch for the person to lie on, ask them to lie on a bed, or even on the floor with a cushion and a few blankets underneath. I actually find working on the floor preferable to a bed, but choose whatever works best for you and is comfortable for the person you are working with.

As the healer, it's important that you feel as comfortable as the person you are working with, so, if working on the bed is most comfortable for them but gives you backache, work on the floor. It will be hard to channel healing energy if you are in pain. That's not to say, of course, it's not possible. As someone with chronic illness, I'm in pretty much constant pain, and I find that healing work is not only possible, but my pain makes me even more aware and conscious of energy. But I think it's safe to say, if you can avoid pain, do so.

Cleanse your room and your crystals

This sounds like an obvious thing to say, but it is of the greatest importance. If your environment or stones are not clean, then your healing efforts will be in vain. They may even become hazardous. Any room that is going to be used for healing needs to be physically as well as energetically clean. I cleanse my healing room in a variety of ways, most often with white sage smoke, in the same way as I would cleanse my crystals (*see Part Two, pages 48–54*). You simply light the sage, blow the flame out, let it smolder, and then walk around the room making sure the smoke gets into every little corner and under every piece of furniture. It is important to have the doors and windows open when you do this so that the negativity can be blown away.

The point of all this preparation is to ensure that when you are ready to bring the person you're working with into the healing space, it is already perfectly prepared and ready to receive them. A room that has been lovingly cleaned, tidied, and space-cleared shows love and attention and makes the person receiving the healing feel valued. In this way, the healing starts before the crystals are laid on the body.

"The intention is to create a space that feels safe, calm, comfortable, and protected."

Preparing the receiver

This layout has been specifically devised to be safe to use on anyone. Although powerful, it is gentle, so you won't need to ask the person you are working with any questions that would normally be asked in a professional crystal healing. It is important to make them feel comfortable; speak to them in a kind manner, calmly and with confidence. Consult the book if you need to; you will soon master the routine. Let the person receiving the healing know that it is fine for them to relax fully, and that you will let them know when it's time for them to get up.

The layout

Ask the person to lie down, making sure that they are comfortable. Ask them to relax as much as possible and to close their eyes. Slowly and gently place each of the crystals on or near to their body, following the positions as described below.

The crystals should be placed on the body in the following order:

1. **Black obsidian** Place between the knees for the base chakra.
2. **Carnelian** Place just below the navel for the sacral chakra.
3. **Yellow jasper** Place above the navel just below the rib cage for the solar plexus chakra.
4. **Green quartz** Place on the middle of the chest for the heart chakra.
5. **Blue quartz** Place on the throat for the throat chakra.
6. **Sodalite** Place in the middle of the forehead just above the eyebrows for the brow chakra.
7. **Clear quartz** Place on the bed or floor just above the top of the head for the crown chakra.

Activation

Once all the crystals are in place, you will need to activate them. Activation is really just like turning on the crystal. Imagine a thread of energy emerging from the stone, spiraling out into the energy of the person receiving the healing. Use one of your index fingers to activate each crystal in turn. Start by pointing your finger at the crystal. Then gradually spiral outward, imagining (or seeing, if you can) the energy of the crystal emerging. Continue to spiral the energy of each crystal out into the energy of the person laying down until all seven crystals have been activated.

Crystal healers use clear quartz points as wands for activation, but your finger will work just as well to start with. You may want to buy yourself two small wands for activation. You need two, because when working with the clear quartz crystal, one wand needs to be in the other hand, pointing downward, to protect you from any negativity that may be picked up during the activation. This is not a risk when using your finger.

Timing

Once all your crystals have been placed on their correct chakras and are nicely activated, it's important to sit back and wait for them to do their work. If this is the first-ever crystal healing for the person you are working with, don't leave them for longer than ten minutes. You can always build up the length of the healing at subsequent sessions. When there is a crystal on each chakra, crystals should never be left on for more than thirty minutes.

Once the time is up, quietly return to your friend and gently begin to remove the crystals in the opposite order in which you placed them, so starting with the crown. It's important to remove the stones gently and slowly, because the body's energy will have linked with the energy of the crystals. We don't want to be ripping the stones off and giving the body a terrible shock.

Before removing the brow stone on the forehead, I find it useful to stroke the hair gently away from the head. This means I don't end up accidentally pulling the hair when removing the stone and causing pain, and it also gives the person a physical sign that I am going to be removing the stone. Often, the brow chakra is one of the most sensitive energy centers, and people can really feel this stone leaving their energy.

Once all the crystals have been removed, gently wake the person by holding their shoulders and speaking their name. As they awake, let them come to for a few minutes, because they will probably be feeling spaced out. Give them a drink of water and let them know that there is no rush for them to get up and back to the real world. Many people like to rest for a few minutes after a crystal healing, so make sure you have allowed time for that.

Once they have left, cleanse your room again using white sage or an incense stick, and cleanse and pack away your crystals (*see Part Two, pages 48–54*).

"*Imagine a thread of energy emerging from the stone, spiraling out into the energy of the person receiving the healing.*"

Using crystal elixirs

A crystal elixir is, in essence, the vibration of a crystal contained in water. It is made by soaking a particular crystal in pure water overnight, causing the vibration of the crystal to be stored and remembered by the molecules of water. It has been proven scientifically, most recently by Professor Emoto (*see Further Reading, page 142*), that water has the ability to hold onto particular vibrations. When we place a crystal in a glass of clean water and let it sit overnight, we are impregnating that water with the energy of the crystal.

Crystal elixirs have a fantastically wide range of applications and are some of the most useful forms of crystal healing. Often, many illnesses

and ailments that would benefit from the energy of a particular crystal are difficult to access. For example, holding a piece of blue agate on your neck when you have a sore throat will help, but gargling with an elixir of blue agate will bring greater and more direct relief.

Other ailments that benefit from crystal elixirs include internal physical problems, such as digestive disorders, kidney infections, and liver weakness. Crystal elixirs have an excellent effect on the emotions, too. People expriencing a broken heart can receive startling results by drinking a small amount of rose quartz elixir each day.

Crystal elixirs can also be used to treat animals, such as cats, dogs, and other pets. Add a drop of the elixir to their drinking water so that they get a regular dose throughout the day.

A clear quartz elixir can be used to space-clear rooms by mixing with essential oils and decanting into a spray-top bottle. This can then be sprayed around a room to clear it of negative energy.

Making your own crystal elixirs

There are two main methods for making elixirs: the direct method and the indirect method.

THE DIRECT METHOD

This can be used to make elixirs from most tumbled (polished) stones.

1. Cleanse your crystal (*see Part Two, pages 48–54*).
2. Place your crystal in a clear glass bowl or glass and cover with spring or mineral water. You can use water from a holy well, but I find plain bottled spring or mineral water to be better, because it has a clearer energy.
3. Let the glass sit overnight in a place where it will not be disturbed. It is important to cover the glass with a dish towel or a piece of cardboard to make sure nothing falls into the elixir overnight.

4. The next day, carefully remove the crystal from the water with a clean plastic or glass utensil. I use either plastic or glass, because energy does not cling to it.
5. Decant the elixir into a spray-top or dosage bottle.

Your elixir will keep for three days, after which time you must throw away whatever is left. I try to make a fresh elixir each day.

THE INDIRECT METHOD

This method is useful for making elixirs from crystals that are either water soluble or harmful to the body if physically ingested. Most crystal reference books should be able to give you information about individual crystals. If in any doubt, use the indirect method. It works just as well as the direct method and it's definitely better to be safe than to feel ill.

Cleanse your crystal (*see Part Two, pages 48–54*).

1. Place your crystal in a small clear glass which you then sit inside another, larger, clear glass bowl.
2. Fill the outer bowl only with fresh spring or mineral water so that no water touches the crystal.
3. Continue as for the direct method, step 3 (*see previous page*).

Dosage

You cannot overdose on an elixir. However, be aware that some elixirs made from crystals with high vibrations, such as azeztulite, phenacite, and even clear quartz, can make you a little light-headed if you take the elixir many times in a short period of time.

It's best to take four drops of elixir four times a day over a period of one month. If you prefer, you can put four drops in a bottle of water and sip it throughout the day.

Using crystals in the home and workplace

Crystals have a wide range of applications beyond healing the human body. They can be used to enhance the energy of any environment. When used correctly and intelligently, crystals can even help to bring wealth, happiness, and harmonious relationships.

Enhancing the energy of a room

Crystals can be used to set up energy grids to change the energy of a room. Crystal grids are geometrical formations of crystals—usually clear quartz points—that work to either enhance or disperse a particular energy. They can also be used to create a safe and protected space as well as to zone out any unwanted energy or influences.

In any work with grids, intention is of the greatest importance. Before you even go out to collect the crystals for your grid, ask yourself why you are setting the grid up. It is essential to the effectiveness of the grid that you have a clear idea of its purpose, and that it is in the forefront of your mind when setting it up. Two examples of useful crystal grids are included below for you to try.

CLEAR QUARTZ AMPLIFYING GRID

This grid uses the Star of David as its base, a symbol of protection for thousands of years. You will need eight small, clear quartz points: six to make the grid up and two to activate it. This grid can be used in either a large area, such as a room or building, or a small area, such as on an altar or small table.

You can use this grid wherever you feel the need for energy to be amplified. I have used it on my altar as well as to enhance the energy of a healing room I worked in, where each of the six points was placed under the carpet when it was being laid. The grid is versatile, but the thing to remember is that it is an amplifying grid. Do not use it where you want to reduce the energy, such as in a bedroom, because it will amplify the energy so much you will have trouble sleeping.

Place the crystal points as directed on the diagram (*see below*), making sure that the points are facing in. Hold one clear quartz point in your dominant hand; you will use this to connect up each of the crystals. Point the quartz in your other hand toward the ground to release any negativity.

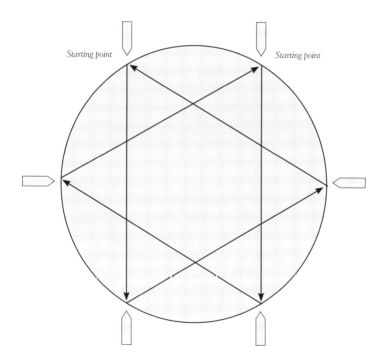

Starting point   *Starting point*

The clear quartz amplifying grid. The arrows show the direction in which the grid needs to be activated.

Once the points are in place, activate them in almost exactly the same way as for the healing layout (*see pages 124–28*). Imagine a thread of energy emerging from each quartz point, spiraling out into the energy of the room. Point one of your quartz points at each crystal, in turn, then gradually spiral outward, imagining (or seeing, if you can) the energy of the crystal being expanded. Then, as each crystal is activated, link its energy to the next crystal, almost as if you were threading one quartz point's energy into the next.

The idea is to link each point together in the order shown, first creating one triangle, then the other, and finally surrounding the grid in a circle of energy, linking one point to the next until you feel the grid is set up. And that is it.

You can also use this grid to increase the vital energy of the food you eat. Often, if I am preparing a meal to be eaten later, I will place the finished dish inside this amplifying grid. Water, as we have learned, also responds well to energy, so when placed in the amplifying grid, it acts like a sponge, soaking up the energy, and drinking this water will then enhance your energy. Sick or injured plants also benefit greatly from being placed inside this grid. However, exercise caution when using the grid with animals and humans. It's best not to perform healings inside the grid unless you have a lot of experience, because the amplification effects can dramatically increase the energy of the crystals inside the grid.

BLACK TOURMALINE PROTECTION GRID

This grid may be useful if you have noisy or disruptive neighbors or any energy that you want to protect yourself from. It all depends what your intention is when setting it up.

You will need a selection of small black tourmaline pieces. The number will depend on how big your grid needs to be. Generally speaking, ten pieces of tourmaline will suffice for even the largest of rooms.

Set the grid up as a circle around whatever space you want to pro-tect. As for the clear quartz amplifying grid (*see page 133*), you will need to use two clear quartz points to activate the grid. This is an easier grid to link up, because it is a simple circle. Hold one of the quartz points in your dominant hand, connecting each of the crystals up, and the second in your other hand, pointing toward the ground to release any negativ-ity. Again, remember always to have your intention at the forefront of your mind when activating the grid.

This grid will work to protect you from anything negative, so it is not necessary, for example, to use extra crystals along the connecting wall of a noisy neighbor. Just set the grid up as normal and it will work well.

Using crystals in conjunction with the feng shui Bagua

One of the most powerful ways to enhance the energy of a room or building is to use crystals in conjunction with the ancient Chinese art of feng shui. Sometimes known as the art of placement, feng shui works on the understanding that everything has an energy, and that it is possible to create an auspicious flow of this energy within your surroundings. When this occurs, everything in life is enhanced: wealth is increased, relationships are productive and harmonious, and a sense of purpose is evident.

Feng shui uses an energy map known as the bagua (pa kua). The diagram on page 136 shows where the energy of each aspect of life resides in any given space. When working with crystals, you place either a crystal amplifying grid or a piece of crystal itself within the corresponding area. For example, if you wanted to enhance your romantic relationship energy, you would place a piece of rose quartz or green quartz in the top right-hand corner of your room or house. Likewise, if you wanted to increase your income, you would create an amplifying grid in the top left-hand corner.

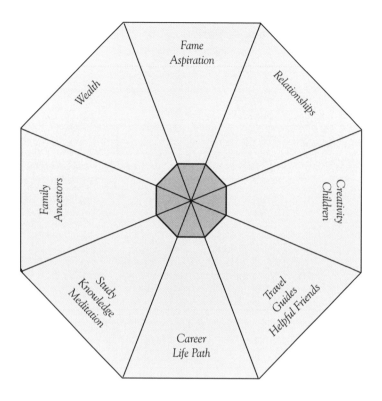

You can identify which crystal is the best one to place in each area from what we have learned about their healing properties. For example, rose quartz is a good crystal to place in your relationships corner, because it is the crystal of love. Likewise, clear quartz is an amplifier of energy as well as a crystal that encourages and supports spiritual growth, so it could be placed as an amplifying grid in the wealth area, or as a single crystal in the spiritual growth area.

Conclusion

It's one thing to devote some time to working through a particular set of meditations but another to keep up the momentum of regular meditation and spiritual practice. Now that you have worked through all of the crystal meditations and learned about the healing qualities of twenty-eight crystals altogether, you have come a long way. Working with crystals is not something that can be started and then suddenly stopped; to live without crystals now probably seems almost impossible. There are some practices you can do on a regular basis to help you stay spiritually connected and build on your good basic knowledge.

Most of my mornings start with a crystal meditation of some kind. The one I use most often simply involves sitting in my quiet space, closing my eyes, and focusing on my breathing, just as we have been doing effectively throughout the book. Once I feel relaxed and calm, I open my eyes and select the first crystal I look at, holding it in my hand and closing my eyes again. I then take a few breaths to realign myself to the energy of the crystal and wait to see where I am taken. Often, I may not go on any particular journey like the ones we have been on in the book. Instead, I will simply feel especially relaxed or will notice a particular part of my physical body feeling better. I stay meditating with my chosen crystal for about fifteen minutes. Then, breathing deeply, I decide to come back to full waking consciousness.

This regular contact with crystals keeps your energy aligned to that of the mineral kingdom. Crystals have a particularly high, pure, and bright vibration, as we have experienced, and to keep our energy keyed in to theirs is of fantastic benefit.

Using crystal elixirs is another way to keep your body's energy running at its optimum frequency. Clear quartz elixir is one of the best immune-boosting remedies I know, and if you're feeling run-down, low, or simply want to stay on top of things, taking a daily dose of clear quartz internally will help greatly (*for information on dosages, see page 131*).

What I hope you have gained from this book is the knowledge and confidence to use crystals in your daily life as you see fit. For example, if you feel a slight irritation building up in your throat, you know that a few drops of blue quartz elixir every couple of hours will help. If you've got an important meeting coming up where you need to stay confident, calm, and in control, you might decide to slip a piece of yellow calcite into your bra or pocket for the day.

Working with crystals is about so much more than simply following prescriptive rules and directions. Now that you know how to communicate with crystals, take the opportunity to get to know the other crystals you may have by meditating with them or simply spending time with them. I hope you find that you become attached to some crystals and less so to others. You may also discover that you sleep best when there is a particular crystal in your bedroom and that you are at your most articulate when you have had a glass of blue calcite elixir. Whatever it is you discover about working and living with crystals, be aware that there are no right or wrong approaches. Some practices may be more effective than others, but all the different ways you interact with your crystals are valid, great, and worthwhile.

Finally, I'm sure I don't need to say this, but love your crystals. Like anything, the more you love, respect, and look after your stones, the more they will do the same for you. Build relationships with them, keep them, give them away, even sell them if you want to, but always love and respect them.

"Crystals have a particularly high, pure, and bright vibration."

Further Reading and Resources

Bourgault, Luc and Eagle, Blue. *The American Indian Secrets of Crystal Healing*, Foulsham, 1996

Croxon, Roger C. *Teach Yourself Crystal Healing*, Teach Yourself Books, 2003

Emoto, Masaru. *Messages from Water: The First Pictures of Frozen Water Crystals*, Hado Publishing, 2003

Gienger, Michael (trans. Mick Astrid). *Crystal Power, Crystal Healing: The Complete Handbook*, Cassell, 2015

Mascaro, Juan. *The Upanishads*, Penguin Books, 2005

Melody. *Love is in the Earth: A Kaleidoscope of Crystals*, Earth-Love Publishing, 1995

Raphaell, Katrina. *Crystal Healing*, Aurora Press, 1987

Raphaell, Katrina. *Crystal Enlightenment*, Aurora Press, 1985

Raven, Hazel. *Crystal Healing: The Complete Practitioner's Guide*. Raven & Co. Publishing, 2000

Sheldrake, Marianna. *The Crystal Healer: A Guide to Understanding Crystals and their Healing Gifts*, C. W. Daniel Co. Ltd, 2009

Hazel Raven's book is a good guide to crystal healing, although it may be somewhat overwhelming for a beginner. Katrina Raphaell's books are essential reading for anyone interested in the more spiritual aspects of crystals. Melody's *Love is in the Earth* is a large encyclopedia of almost all minerals and a classic resource for learning about the spiritual and metaphysical properties of crystals. Although I don't agree with everything in it, it remains an excellent textbook for the spiritual study of crystals. Masaru Emoto's groundbreaking book contains photographic evidence that water absorbs energy. All of Dr. Dean Radin's books are fascinating and offer a scientific framework for understanding how crystals work. *The Conscious Universe* is perhaps a good place to start.

About the Author

Kate Tomas is a renowned psychic, witch, and crystal healer who works to awaken people to their infinite potential and help them tap into their innate gifts. Her compassion, wisdom, and world-class education have all earned her the reputation as one of the most sought-after magickal practitioners working today. She holds a doctoral degree in philosophical theology from the University of Oxford and lives between London and New York with her spouse Ames, two rescue cats, George and Gershwin, and a rescue chihuahua, Dominic.

Picture Credits

ShutterStockphoto.Inc 14–15 May_Chanikran; 22 Steve Rawlings/Debut Art 2007; 26 avesun; 29 sondem; 31 vivver; 36 coka; 42–43 Maria Bocharova; 51 Coral Antler Creative; 56–57 Edalin Photography; 64–65 Visions-AD; 67 Martinho Smart; 71 Dr Morley Read; 75 Alexandra Theile; 81 Grisha Bruev; 83 1000 Words; 91 Lisa Verrecchia; 97 vitalinka; 99 melnikof; 105 zwiebackesser; 107 sishasakprachum; 113 Jay Ondreicka; 115 Lava 4 images; 121 IgorZh; 122–23 Nikki Zalewski and Triff; 129 stockcreations; 137 Monika Wisniewska.

ACKNOWLEDGMENTS

Managing Director *Lisa Dyer*
Managing Editor *Nicolette Kaponis*
Proofreader *Nicky Gyopari*
Designer *Brazzle Atkins*
Production *Sarah Rooney*